Science, Pseudo-science, Non-sense, and Critical Thinking

Science, Pseudo-science, Non-sense, and Critical Thinking shines an unforgiving light on popular and lucrative "miraculous" practices that promise to offer answers during times of trouble. Throughout the book, the authors unfold the fallacies underlying these practices, as well as consumers' need and desire to believe in them.

Adopting a scientific approach, the book critically evaluates research into cold-reading practices, such as those that claim to be able to communicate with the afterlife or possess supernatural powers, before considering a range of pseudo-sciences including graphology and polygraph interrogation, exposing the pretensions of these practices in a clear and logical fashion. The book seeks to encourage critical thinking throughout, asking whether there is any scientific evidence to support these practitioners' abilities to supply us with reliable answers, and discussing the various factors that comprise the psychological mechanism of belief.

Written in a fluent and accessible style, *Science, Pseudo-science, Non-sense, and Critical Thinking* is aimed at interested professionals and the public at large.

Marianna Barr studied English and Comparative Literature. She has written and translated poetry as well as translated numerous theoretical books, essays, and short stories.

Gershon Ben-Shakhar is a Professor Emeritus in the Department of Psychology, Hebrew University of Jerusalem, and a leading expert in the psychophysiological detection of deception.

Science, Pseudo-science, Non-sense, and Critical Thinking

Why the Differences Matter

BY Marianna Barr and Gershon Ben-Shakhar

Translated from Hebrew by Marianna Barr

LONDON AND NEW YORK

First published 2019
by Routledge
2 Park Square, Milton Park, Abingdon, Oxon OX14 4RN

and by Routledge
711 Third Avenue, New York, NY 10017

Routledge is an imprint of the Taylor & Francis Group, an informa business

© 2019 Marianna Barr and Gershon Ben-Shakhar

The right of Marianna Barr and Gershon Ben-Shakhar to be identified as authors of this work has been asserted by them in accordance with sections 77 and 78 of the Copyright, Designs and Patents Act 1988.

All rights reserved. No part of this book may be reprinted or reproduced or utilised in any form or by any electronic, mechanical, or other means, now known or hereafter invented, including photocopying and recording, or in any information storage or retrieval system, without permission in writing from the publishers.

Trademark Notice: Product or corporate names may be trademarks or registered trademarks and are used only for identification and explanation without intent to infringe.

Translated from the *The Deceptive Machine: Mysticism and Pseudo-Science in Personality Assessment and Prediction*

Published by Matar Publishing House, 2014

British Library Cataloguing-in-Publication Data
A catalogue record for this book is available from the British Library.

Library of Congress Cataloging-in-Publication Data
A catalog record for this title has been requested

ISBN: 978-1-138-30076-7 (hbk)
ISBN: 978-1-138-30103-0 (pbk)
ISBN: 978-0-203-73289-2 (ebk)

Typeset in Sabon
by codeMantra

Visit the eResources: www.routledge.com/9781138301030

Contents

Preface ix
Acknowledgments xv

Introduction 1

1 You have great unfulfilled potential:
 cold (psychic) reading 5
 What is cold reading? 5
 Tarot cards 8
 Cold reading and psychological science 10
 How does it work? 14
 Why does it work? 19
 How much does it cost? 23
 Bibliography 32

2 "They love you and you know that": astrology 35
 An overview of astrology 35
 Astrology and science 37
 Bibliography 44

3 Show me your handwriting and
I'll tell you who you are: graphology 45
Science and Pseudo science 46
History of graphology 49
The use of graphology 52
Is handwriting truly a mirror of our personality? 53
The "theoretical" approach 54
The "empirical" approach 56
The validity of graphology 58
   Comparison to reality 59
   Contamination of handwritten samples with
      biographical data 61
   The difficulty in quantifying graphologists'
      evaluations 61
Bibliography 69

4 Pinocchio's nose: the truth behind the
lie detector 71
*Oops, an innocent man has been condemned to
   life imprisonment* 71
Lying, honesty, and the desire to tell them apart 72
The truth will out: a brief history of the polygraph 76
The relevant/irrelevant questions test 77
The comparison question test (CQT) 78
The directed lie test 86
The concealed information test (CIT) 86
*The CQT versus the CIT – where is the scientific
   basis?* 90
Accuracy of the CQT versus the CIT 100
*The use of the polygraph in screening and
   classification processes* 103
*The use of integrity tests as an alternative
   to the CQT* 109
Bibliography 112

5 "Since man cannot live without miracles, he will provide himself with miracles of his own making": the belief in practices based on cold reading, mysticism, and pseudo-science 115
   The need to believe 115
   Abuse of the need to believe 116
   Popular beliefs 117
   Bias in human judgment 118
   The clients' belief 121
   The burden of doubt and incertitude 121
   The need to remove personal responsibility 123
   The influence of the Barnum effect 124
   Bias for positive evidence 124
   Social and cultural influences (conformity) 125
   Shifting the burden of proof 128
   The practitioners' belief 128
      The confirmation bias 130
      Illusory validity 136
   Bibliography 138

6 A final word 141

Index 143

Preface

The practices reviewed in this book that fall under the category of "cold reading" have always put me off. My antagonism stemmed from using simple logic, and also from an intuition that these practices have no stronghold in reality. Every time friends or relatives would tell me with glittering eyes of a cold reader who not only told them what they had already known regarding their lives or tribulations but also foretold their future, I felt rage and embarrassment. Time and again I wondered why in our modern world, which provides us with so many means of assistance and support – modern medicine, psychiatry, psychotherapy, counselors, and other professionals who have undergone many years of rigorous training and qualifications – so many people, including highly learned and talented ones, resort to seeking advice and comfort from astrologists, cold readers, and their like.

When I met Gershon, who is an experimental psychologist, I found out that among his fields of study were graphology and the polygraph, of which I knew nothing at all. Gershon exposed me to his studies as well as to the principles of experimental science. I was brought up on the principles of Humanities – English and comparative literature, translation – and I have also educated myself through intensive and extensive reading of philosophy, theory in general, psychoanalysis, and art. Over time, Gershon and I have influenced each other a lot. We have learnt from our own experience with each other about the human tendency to dismiss the different in order to solidify our own view, and so very often we risk throwing the baby out with the bath water.

When we both retired from Hebrew University – Gershon from teaching and his other administrative duties, for he continues to conduct research and supervise students, and I from my administrative position, which left me free to pursue my desires since always to write and translate – Gershon thought that the time had come to join forces in a creative symbiosis and produce a popular book on mysticism and pseudo-science. In the summer of 2010, we spent a blissful sabbatical in Maastricht, Holland, during which I read numerous books and articles relevant to the writing of the book, including those written by Gershon himself. The more I read, the more my and our enthusiasm grew, both for sharing our insights between us as well as sharing them with others.

In contrast to popular belief, critical thinking in nonexperimental sciences and critical thinking in experimental sciences are not opposing forces. They may complement and enhance each other in very creative ways, as we ourselves have done when writing this book and we try to do in our daily lives. Many are the fields and phenomena that are not based on scientific principles and do not cease to instruct us and enrich our lives in unimaginable ways: art, literature, poetry (which have rules and theories of their own that change over time, but are not based on scientifically obtained evidence), various psychological treatments (some evidence-based, some not), traveling in the world, professional and personal relationships, and life itself. They all inspire us and arouse in us both positive and negative feelings.

However, there is a time for wandering in feeling and in thought, and there is a time for relying only on facts based on controlled scientific experiments and on accumulated knowledge and experience. When we are forced to make crucial decisions regarding our health, our professional future, and maybe even our very existence, we had better embark on a rational process of decision-making. As to all the practices we cover in our book, I am convinced that even if science and scientific tools are not perfect (what is?) and may not provide answers to all the questions troubling us, in the twenty-first century, they remain our most objective, reliable tool.

Our approach in this book has followed critical thinking and the principles of experimental science, and we truly hope that we have succeeded not only in explicating the difference between science and pseudo-science but also in endowing the readers with some tools for critical judgment and critical thinking, even if they will ultimately follow one of the reviewed practices in the hope that "it helps even if you do not believe"! If much of the demand for such practices is the result of the difficulty of coping with uncertainty and lack of control over our lives, then we assure our readers that one of the clear benefits of critical thinking is precisely the acquisition of some measure of control over our future, and most certainly the responsibility of our decisions.

Finally, working with Gershon has been a true gift. Perhaps if we had competed for the same territory, we would have torn each other's hair, but as it was, this book could not have been written by Gershon alone and certainly not by me. To what extent our project has been successful, we let the readers judge.

Marianna Barr

Many years ago, I was asked to give my expert opinion on a case.[1] Two apartments owned by a businessman – whom I shall call Mr. Smith – caught fire. Mr. Smith sued his insurance company. The insurance company demanded that he take a polygraph test. Since he was totally ignorant of the type of polygraph test administered in such cases, he consulted with his attorney who, in turn, advised him to approach a polygraph agency on his own without informing the insurance company, and so he did. When the polygraph agency informed him that he was found truthful, he returned to the insurance company to tell them that he agreed to take the test. To his amazement, the polygraph examiners hired by the insurance company found him deceitful. What is there to do when we are faced with two opposing results? Mr. Smith looked for a third polygraph agency hoping that its conclusion would constitute a majority in his favor. But to his great dismay, this agency found the end result "inconclusive". And the story goes on – a test administered by a fourth polygraph agency concluded that Mr. Smith was truthful in regard to one of the apartments and deceitful in regard to the other.

Cases such as this have prompted me to pursue the applicative implications of my fields of study. Throughout my academic career, beginning in the 1970s, I have engaged in two main fields of study: cognitive psychophysiology and psychological tests. At the outset, my psychophysiological studies centered on the study of "orienting response", that is, behavioral and physiological responses to changes in the environment or to new and unexpected stimuli. We are all familiar with a situation in which we are at peace reading a book when the telephone suddenly rings. In such a situation, we turn our head almost automatically in the direction of the ringing. This constitutes a behavioral response. Concurrently, it is possible to measure a series of physiological responses during this occurrence, such as deceleration in our heartbeat, a breathing pose, and a widening of the eye pupil diameter.

Psychophysiological studies show that orienting responses increase especially when the unexpected stimulus has special significance for us (for example, when someone calls out our name unexpectedly). Soon enough, I was captivated by the idea that it is possible to use the orienting response in order to diagnose concealed information or information that we have trouble expressing verbally. This is how I began investigating the psychophysiological detection of information, or what is commonly known as the "polygraph" (lie detector). Already, at the beginning of my academic career, I realized that the polygraph method employed by the police and other investigative agencies (as a tool to detect lies and not conceal information) is problematic and devoid of any logical, theoretical, or scientific basis.

Indeed, from the beginning of the 1970s, I published with my colleagues a series of scholarly articles rigorously criticizing the use of the polygraph for detecting lies or liars. During that time, the polygraph had many enthusiasts not only in the police force but also in the district attorney's office, where the possibility of employing it not just as an investigative tool but also as admissible evidence in criminal procedures was seriously considered. This idea prompted me and my colleagues, Shlomo Kugelmass and Israel Lieblich, to step out of the academic ivory tower and do our utmost to convince the legal system to abandon this dangerous idea. Our efforts led to the establishment of the Cohen Committee (which we mention in the book), which concluded its deliberations in a categorical negation of the possibility of granting the polygraph test results admissibility in a criminal court of law.

In my study of psychological tests and their applications to objectives such as diagnostics, screening, and classification, I encountered very problematic uses of these tests. One such example was the widespread practice of graphology in Israel for the benefit of personnel selection as well as in the context of population admission to new settlements. Together with my colleagues Maya Bar-Hillel and Yoram Bilu, I proceeded to conduct a series of experiments on graphology which yielded a few articles exposing the inanity of the use of graphology. However, despite our studies and the many articles we published on these two topics, the world is what it is and these two industries continue to flourish.

For many years, my wife Marianna Barr urged me to step out of the ivory tower once more and write a book approachable to all that would reveal to the public at large the fact that popularity does not make right and that popular practices – such as polygraph tests and graphology – are not in the least based on scientific principles, are totally without validity, and constitute a good example of "pseudo-science". Unfortunately, I had to refuse, for I am not skilled in non-academic writing. Time passed, and eventually, I proposed to Marianna the following collaboration: I would provide her with the relevant material, and she would use her writing skills to write a book. She came on board without hesitation, the result of which was the publication of the book in Israel, in Hebrew. During the past year, she also translated the book for its publication in English. For its current edition, we have added some information as well as omitted other that seemed redundant to us, as is the case with new updated editions. I am so very grateful to her for all the work she has put in this endeavor. For the readers, I hope that – besides learning that I have a gifted spouse – after learning how these practices operate, they will refrain from seeking solace or rescue through them.

Gershon Ben-Shakhar

Note

1 To protect the people involved, I have altered a few identifying items that are not essential to the argument.

Acknowledgments

We are extremely grateful to our friends who remarked on individual chapters of the original Hebrew manuscript while we were writing it – Yoram Bilu, Maya Bar-Hillel, Ram Frost – and to those who read the manuscript upon completion – Shlomo Angel, Naama Ben-Shakhar, Shiloh de Baer, Jacob Metzer, Shai Satran. Their comments and suggestions undoubtedly contributed to its improvement. We also thank Hana Lapidot, Sandra Meiri, and Lotem Elber for their useful remarks. Regarding the English version of the book, our deepest gratitude goes to David Bearison for his meticulous reading of the entire manuscript, his corrections, and suggestions.

We cannot refrain from mentioning the steady love and support that accompany our lives provided by all the amazing members of our family: our generation – Sandra and Benny Meiri, Kochevet Ben-Shakhar; the younger generation – Yuval, Naama, Tal, Tamar; the youngest ones – Amir, Libi, Ori, Carmel – the shining lights of our lives.

Introduction

Most of us, at one time or another in our lives, especially in times of trouble or uncertainty, have sought solace, whether out of anguish or out of curiosity, in various clairvoyants, future tellers, palm readers or card readers. If it was loneliness we were suffering from and were desperately looking for love or companionship, we might have received an advice which, out of context, would have seemed completely groundless and even ridiculous. But given our dire circumstances, it seemed so little to do for so much to gain. And so, we did not flee from the scene but remained put, filled with awe and wonder at the gifts that had just been bestowed on us. Here is an example of an advice given to a woman seeking the love of her life:

> Take a sheet of blank paper, one red marker, one envelope, your favorite perfume, your favorite red lipstick, and 5 or 6 fresh red rose petals. Use the red marker to write down the qualities that you are looking for in a new love, being specific and realistic. Do not use names! Give the paper a spray or dab of your perfume, then fold it into the envelope. Hold the rose petals in your hand, and picture yourself with your ideal mate. Let yourself feel how happy you would be. Put the petals into the envelope with the paper, and seal the envelope. With a little lipstick on your lips, plant a big kiss

on the outside of the envelope. Keep the envelope in a safe spot, and do not open it. Once you've found your new lover, you can simply throw it away or burn it. Just don't open it.[1]

We are continually exposed to various methods and practices claiming to provide us with answers, comfort, healing, the truth, and even information regarding our future. This book examines two such categories of practices: The first one includes practices that have no scientific claims but are extremely popular, and, as we shall see, their practitioners make a fortune at the expense of our credulity and naivety. These practitioners claim to know detailed information about people or predict their future based on the status of the stars, supernatural powers, and/or communication with the dead. Since all of these practices are based on identical principles, it is customary to classify them under the category "cold reading". The second category of practices examined in this book does indeed claim to have scientific validity but, in reality, as we hope to show, are merely pseudo-scientific. Under this category, we examine the use of graphology (handwriting analysis) and the more popular polygraph investigative method. Albeit their popularity and the faith that they inspire in people, apart from the fact that they are very lucrative industries, the public at large is not familiar with the way these practices operate nor with what they are based on. Is there any evidence that supports their claims to provide reliable answers? Is there any solid basis to the scientific claims made by polygraph and graphology practitioners?

The first two chapters of the book are an in-depth analysis of the dynamics that exists between cold readers and their clients, and they demonstrate how each one of us may acquire the various skills of cold reading, in other words, "superpowers". The third chapter is a thorough analysis of graphology and its reliability, validity, and scientific basis. It also aims to uncover the secret of its charm and, as a result, its popularity. The fourth chapter is an in-depth examination of the polygraph, or as it is often referred to, the "lie detector".[2] The polygraph features almost daily both in the news and in fictitious shows and films as a magic tool possessing the ability to distinguish between liars and truth speakers, be it within the context of criminal cases or within the context of screening and classifying employees entrusted with tasks or duties of a sensitive nature. We do not content ourselves with exposing only the lie behind the lie detector, but we also expose the damages that this popular method yields. Indeed, in this context, we would like to point out that contrary to graphology, let alone astrology and other practices of cold reading, as far as the polygraph goes, *there does exist* a method of investigation whose scientific validity has been demonstrated, but as we shall see, it is unfortunately not very common.

We admit that our aim is to show that the king is naked, in other words to expose the fallacies at the heart of these practices. The scientific claim that accompanies graphology and the polygraph is undoubtedly the reason why these practices have been examined through rigorous tools by scientists around the world, and we make use of this vast corpus of research to base our arguments. We hope that these two chapters will provide a kind of tailwind to aid people to refuse to have their handwriting examined by graphologists or be interrogated through the more common, popular, polygraph interrogation method. We hope to demonstrate that the popularity of these practices does not attest to their validity.

The common ground to all the practices we examine, the ones with no scientific pretense and the ones based on pseudo-science, is faith – the belief in them – both on the part of the practitioners as well as on the part of the clients. The last chapter in this book is therefore devoted to the various causes of the clients' belief that these practices may indeed be a source of comfort and aid.

The clients' belief is essential to the existence of these practices; the practitioners' (astrologers, palm readers, graphologists, and polygraphists) belief is not vital but is, of course, a helping factor. Hence, in this chapter, we also aim to understand not only why the clients believe in the powers of the cold reading to supply reliable answers but also why many of the practitioners believe in their merchandise and are so eager to sell it, despite the lack of any sustaining empirical evidence.

We hope that our readers will enjoy the book and benefit from it as well as adopt a more critical way of thinking – which is indeed the ultimate goal of the book – when faced with the practices examined in it.

Finally, throughout the book, we tend to use the masculine pronoun to facilitate the reader's flow, but the matters apply, of course, to both genders.

Notes

1 See https://www.free-witchcraft-spells.com/free-easy-love-spells.html
2 We find it worth noting, especially given the fact that this is an English translation of the original book written in Hebrew and published in Israel, that the polygraph's Hebrew name is 'the truth machine'.

1

You have great unfulfilled potential
Cold (psychic) reading

What is cold reading?

We have tried to track the term "cold reading", but our efforts have proved of no avail. It could be that the term comes from the alleged communication with spirits and the dead, who belong to the "cold world". The reading refers, of course, to the interpretations, assessments, and predictions supplied by the various readers.

The American psychologist Ray Hyman – the most important researcher of cold reading (or psychic reading) and the paranormal, and an amateur magician – relates that during his college days, he used to make a living from palmistry and magic. When he started working as a palm reader, he did not believe in this practice but knew that in order to be able to sell his services he needed to pretend that he was a believer, which he did. As a result of his success with the readings and the positive feedback he received from his clients, he became, in due course, a firm believer of the practice. One day, a friend of Hyman, of whom he thought highly, proposed to him an interesting experiment: to purposely inverse the reading of what the lines in the palms "showed". Hyman tried it with several clients, and to his amazement, the readings were not any less successful! This incident was the beginning of his interest in the enormous psychological powers that influence both readers and clients. According to Hyman, cold reading constitutes a "prototype to how compelling, but false, beliefs come about".

Cold reading is a procedure during which the readers are able to convince strangers they have never met before that they are familiar with everything there is to know about them, including their personality traits, problems, and dilemmas. As a rule, such a reading is comprised from very general statements that can be applied to almost anyone; nevertheless, it provides clients with information that seems to be tailored to their conditions and personalities.

Hyman identifies three main reasons for the success of cold reading:

> (1) ... we all are basically more alike than different; (2) ... our problems are generated by the same major transitions of birth, puberty, work, marriage, children, old age, and death; (3) ... with the exception of curiosity seekers and troublemakers, people come to a character reader because they need someone to listen to their conflicts typically involving love, money, and health.

But the cold readers go far beyond these common denominators. Indeed, they make meticulous detectives. They gather as much information as they can, regarding the clients prior to their encounter with them. If the meeting is set in a telephone conversation, the readers can extract information from various sources, especially today in the age of the internet and various social networks. In addition, the readers rely on very good memory and an acute sense of observation. During the meeting itself, they examine the clients carefully: the study of their clothes – style, neatness, cost, age – provides a good insight into their socioeconomic level, measure of extraversion or introversion, measure of conservatism, and so on. Hyman illustrates this aspect through a story told by a well-known magician in the 1930s: a young woman in her late twenties or early thirties visited a character reader. She was wearing expensive jewels, a wedding band, but a cheap-looking black dress. The reader noticed that the shoes she was wearing were being advertised at that time for people with foot problems. By means of these observations alone, the reader managed to amaze his client. He understood that she was there either with a romantic or a financial problem. From the black dress, he concluded that she had lost her husband not too long ago. From the expensive jewels, he inferred that her financial situation had been better before his passing, and the cheap material of her dress and the orthopedic shoes provided the proof that he had left her in a bad financial condition and that she had to work to earn her living. All of these led the skillful reader to describe the woman's dilemma quite correctly: she had met a man who had proposed to her, she wanted to accept in order to better her dire financial condition but felt guilty to marry so soon after her husband's death. The reader, of course, told her what she longed to hear: that she could marry at once.

Simple, readily available data – such as age and gender – are also a good clue for sizing up the clients. The Israeli psychologist and anthropologist Yoram Bilu relates the story of a rabbi healer whom he met during one of his studies who told him how it is possible to guess with high probability the problems of the women seeking his help: the young ones come with romantic problems, the middle-aged ones with problems related to their spouses or children, and the old ones with health problems.

The physical characteristics of the clients – weight, posture, body movements, and looks – also provide good clues. Other good "tellers" are the figure of speech, language use, and eye contact. The crucial information that the readers extract from the initial examination of the client narrows down considerably the number of categories into which they may be classified. Knowledge of actuarial and statistical data regarding subcultures and populations, as we will see later on, also provides the basis for making an accurate assessment of the client. And the dynamics of the reading is such that what the reader is ignorant of or wrong about, the client will immediately complete or correct.

The aim of the readers is to arrive as quickly as possible to the heart of the problem bothering the clients. On the basis of the initial assessment, they offer several directions, which they deliver in very general terms, while closely examining the clients' reactions, such as eye movements, expansion of the pupils, and other bodily reactions. When the readers are on the right track, they will receive confirmation from the clients' reactions. If the clients' reactions do not encourage the readers to continue their line of thought, the latter will change their course immediately. The clients may also react verbally, negating or reaffirming the statements, mostly without being aware of it at all.

At this point, the clients are already convinced that by some miracle, the readers have gained direct access to their innermost thoughts and feelings, and their defense mechanisms weaken. Very often, the clients open their hearts to the readers who are very good listeners, and share with them the problems that worry them. Ultimately, the readers supply the clients with an assessment that reflects nothing more than the information they had received from the clients, and, as we have pointed out, without the latter being aware of it. And they do it in a way that astounds the clients and makes them feel like an open book.

Tarot cards

Since there is sufficient literature on the history of tarot cards and their functions,[1] we do not aim here to review a detailed history of them, but rather discuss their use in cold reading, since they seem to be the bread and butter of this practice. But their validity in character reading or future predictions is as well founded as is the use of the crystal ball.

Tarot (originally French-named) cards are a set of cards originally designed as a game. But over time, a popular belief has been adopted by many that these cards can help us predict the future. To begin, we adopt Paul Huson's chronology of the tarot from their inception in Europe:

> In the fourteenth century the Mamlûk playing cards were introduced into Europe and were used for games. European decks generally comprised four suits, each headed by a king and one or two ministers. The ministers evolved into knights, knaves, and queens. In the fifteenth century 22 pictorial trump cards were added to the Tarot deck in Italy, which became the standard deck, and painted cards were created for the nobility. In the sixteenth century printed Tarot were produced in Florence, Bologna and Ferrara and they spread

to France, Switzerland, Belgium and Spain. Caption and roman numerals were added to the trumps. At this stage, Tarot cards were widely used for card games. But by the eighteenth century the Tarot cards acquired, in addition to their game function, the function of cartomancy (practice of foretelling the future using cards), and from the nineteenth century onwards – during which periods Hebrew Kabbalistic symbolism and astrology were incorporated into the Tarot – the cards began to be used exclusively for cartomancy.

(p. xv)

In addition to serving as a tool for future predictions, in the twentieth century, tarot also began to serve as a tool for inner observation and reflection, for a better understanding of personality components and inclinations. The Swiss psychoanalyst Carl G. Jung saw in tarot a representation of what he termed "archetypes", that is, basic types or modes of thought prevailing in what he termed "collective unconscious", emanating from the accumulated human experience at large. Thus, the emperor's card, for instance, will symbolize the ultimate patriarch or the father figure. Indeed, there are psychotherapists – in particular, Jungian – who use tarot cards as a kind of projective technique. The clients are required to choose the cards with which they feel most affinity. Some therapists encourage their clients to clarify their situations or their relationships with others through the figures or the situations reflected in the cards.

But the idea that we may produce answers to essential questions occupying our minds and time through an arbitrary choice of cards is so preposterous that it is not really necessary to disqualify it through scientifically based evidence. Indeed, there are almost no such experiments in existence. The ones that do exist were conducted in similar methods that Shawn Carlson employed in his study on astrology (see Chapter 2 on astrology). Equally ridiculous seem to us the "basic instructions" outlined by the Israeli Tarot reader Gidi Gilboa in his book. Judge for yourselves:

Try to avoid eating for two to three hours before you open the cards.
Try to shower or purge yourself before opening the cards.

Turn to the cosmic powers (according to your view) and ask them to help you in the card reading.

Try using only your left hand in handling the cards.

If you wish to draw positive energies to the cards, light a candle or incense in the room.

Greet the clients cordially and offer them a drink.

Sit with your back to the North and seat the clients on the opposite end of the table facing you.

As we pointed out, various mystics and cold readers use tarot cards extensively. But in contrast to the psychotherapist, who may use the cards in the service of a therapeutic process and treat a card and its representation symbolically, the various cold readers perform a literal reading of the card, and this is a world of difference. We believe that the use of accessories such as tarot cards, a crystal ball, tea leaves, and dried coffee serves mainly to create the illusion that there is an independent, "objective" instrument that guides the reader. It also buys the readers more time to observe and assess their customers carefully.

It is our impression that astrology and tarot card reading are the most widespread practices in the lucrative business of future predictions, albeit mystics use other peculiar aids in their readings as well, such as tea leaves, turned cups of coffee once the liquid has dried and left traces of the dried content, and palmistry. All of them are based on the same psychological mechanisms reviewed above, which is also why they are all referred to by the generic name "cold reading".

Cold reading and psychological science

As we have seen, cold readers are quite swift, skilled people. But the truly astonishing thing about cold reading is that even readers lacking any talents or skills can persuade people that they have deciphered their "true" personality. All they need to do is to propose a reasonable hypothesis – and the rest will be done by the clients themselves. And it is possible to achieve a considerable level of success also when an invariable personality description is used, known in the psychological literature as "stock spiel" – one rule for all.

The first experiment documented in the psychological literature that demonstrates how a stock spiel works was conducted in 1949 by Bertram Forer with the aid of his "Introduction to Psychology" students. Forer distributed to 39 students a standard personality test. After a week had passed, he gave each one of the students a uniform personality description – that may also be termed "profile" – which, they were told, was drawn up from their tests. It included very general amorphous statements which Forer put together from an astrology book he had purchased at a newspaper stand. The students were asked to rank the degree of suitability of the profile they had received to their personality on a scale from 0 (no match) to 5 (perfect match). The average grade obtained was 4.26. Of his 39 students, 16 (41%) ranked the profile as a perfect description of their personality. Only four ranked it under 4. This experiment became a standard exercise in the "Introduction to Psychology" course in many universities across the world, and students have continued to produce similar results. This phenomenon is known in the psychological literature as the "Forer Effect" or the "Barnum Effect". P.T. Barnum was a businessman, an impresario, and a circus man who used to employ this method in his performances.

In an article published in 1955, American psychologist Norman Sundberg provides examples of profiles that demonstrate the Barnum Effect well. Here is one such example that may suit any male student:

> You are a person who is very normal in his attitudes .... You get along well without effort .... You are neither overly conventional nor overly individualistic. Your prevailing mood is one of optimism and constructive effort, and you are not troubled by periods of depression ....

Sundberg found that female students responded even more readily to the following sketch:

> You appear to be a cheerful, well-balanced person. You may have some alternation of happy and unhappy moods, but they are not extreme now. You have few or no problems

with your health .... Your interests are wide. You are fairly self-confident and usually think clearly.

In one experiment, Sundberg distributed to 44 students the Minnesota Multiphasic Personality Inventory (MMPI). This is a standard personality test designed to diagnose psychopathologies in adults and has been employed as a central tool in personality research. It was and has remained one of the most important tools in the toolbox of clinical psychologists. Two psychologists, experienced in analyzing MMPI results, drafted a personality description for each student based on the MMPI results. Then, each student received two profiles: one drafted by the psychologist, and the other uniform one, invented and drafted in very general terms. When they were asked to choose the profile closer to their personality, of the 44 students, 26 (59%) chose the invented one. This showed that a general, invented description may be perceived as a better description than the one drafted by professional psychologists and based on one of the better assessment tools in psychology. In the 1970s, the American psychologist Charles Snyder and his colleagues conducted a number of experiments in order to further investigate the Barnum Effect. In one of these experiments, they presented all their students with the following stock spiel:

> Some of your aspirations tend to be pretty unrealistic. At times you are extroverted, affable, sociable, while at other times you are introverted, wary and reserved. You have found it unwise to be too frank in revealing yourself to others ... At times you have serious doubts as to whether you have made the right decision or done the right thing. Disciplined and controlled on the outside, you tend to be worrisome and insecure on the inside.
>
> Your sexual adjustment has presented some problems for you ... You have a great deal of unused capacity which you have not turned to your advantage. You have a tendency to be critical of yourself. You have a strong need for other people to like you ... and to admire you.

The experimental group received the above description, and the participants were told that it had been drafted to match their personalities. In the control group, the participants received the same stock spiel but were told that this is a general description that may suit anyone. In both groups, the participants were asked to rank the proximity of the description to their personality, on a scale of 1 to 5 (1 = very weak, 2 = weak, 3 = average, 4 = good, 5 = excellent). In the control group, the typical result obtained was a ranking of 3 to 4 – average to good. In the experimental group, the typical ranking went up to 4.5 – good to excellent.

Another experiment included three conditions. Participants in the control condition received the stock spiel and were told that this was a general description that may suit anyone. In the two experimental conditions, participants were asked to provide personal information to an astrologer and then received the same stock spiel that was allegedly based on an astrological reading. While in the first experimental condition, they provided only the year and month of their birth, in the second experimental condition, they were requested to provide also the exact day of their birth. The results revealed an average rating of 3.24 in the control condition (slightly above average), an average rating of 3.76 in the first experimental condition (slightly beyond good), and a much higher average rating of 4.38 (good to excellent) in the second experimental condition.

From these experiments, we learn that the acceptability of the stock spiel increases when (1) the readers are perceived as sources who know what they are doing, (2) the tool or evaluation device inspire confidence, (3) irrelevant items or pieces of information (such as date of birth) accompany the procedure, and (4) the clients are led to believe that the description has been tailored to their personality. The more these conditions are present, the more the clients – and possibly the readers, too – are stricken by a strong illusion of uniqueness, in that the clients are convinced that the description matches their personality exclusively.

Since the 1980s, the experiments on the Barnum Effect have gradually decreased, because the result obtained in the early experiments cannot be altered either by time or by other variables. Various scholars offer different interpretations to the Barnum Effect. Some claim that the main reason for the high acceptability of the Barnum Effect is precisely its universality – its general terms and suitability to most people. Others contend that the explanation is more complex and that some items in the Barnum description are highly acceptable, for they enable the participants to project onto them their own personal interpretations. Other statements are perceived as valid because they include flattering characteristics.

It is worth noting that a great part of the scientific literature regarding the Barnum Effect assumes that people do not possess an in-depth knowledge of their own personality and that their naivety is what drives them to see in the stock spiel an accurate unique description of their personality. But other scholars are totally opposed to this view and accentuate that people tend to accept the stock spiel precisely because it is close to their personality and because they lack the basis for comparison. We will return to this point later on.

How does it work?

The Barnum Effect and the studies concerned with it apply to a situation in which there is no direct interaction between the cold readers and the clients. In most cold reading situations, the cold readers who lean a great deal on the Barnum Effect benefit also from the added interaction with their clients and the additional data which, as we have pointed out, the readers may obtain prior to the readings. The laboratory studies we have described have been successful in isolating many of the factors responsible for convincing the clients that an invariable description of personality (a "stock spiel") is an accurate unique description of their personality. But the success of the reading depends also on what we may call or refer to as "the directing/staging of the scene". Hyman drafts 13 of what he terms "the rules of the game", which we have summarized into 11 because of some very close similarities:

1. Self-confidence. By means of an external conduct that emanates confidence, it is possible to "sell" to most clients even a bad reading. As we have seen, the lab studies support this. Many readings are perceived as correct because they rely on descriptions that fit most people. But readings that might be discarded as inaccurate are also accepted if the readers are perceived as "professionals". Alas, one of the dangers of this

behavior is that it may result in the readers' own belief (as it happened to Hyman himself) that they are indeed capable of deciphering a personality or predicting the future.

In this context, we would like to refer our readers to an interview conducted by the journalist David Frost with the well-known director and actor Orson Wells a few years ago. In this interview, Wells relates in a very succinct and amusing way an experience with cold reading. He emphasizes how the readers – and brings himself as an example when he decided to devote a whole day disguised as a reader endowed with supernatural powers – begin to believe, during the course of the reading process, that they indeed possess such powers.[2]

2. Creative use of the latest statistical abstracts, polls, and surveys. These data provide information on the typical problems characterizing the various subgroups of our society. For example, if the readers can determine which part of town the clients are from, the size of the town they grew up in, their parents' occupation, their religious, ethnic, and educational background, and their age, then they already possess a great deal of information through which they may predict with a high probability the clients' political partiality, their positions on many other issues, and so on.

3. Attractive staging of the location. The readers must emanate modesty as far as their talent is concerned and not brag with extreme or excessive claims and appearances. Clients may be taken aback by such behavior. The reading has to be delivered in a way that does not pose a threat to the clients, in a way that convinces the clients that the readers are delving into their character and, at the same time, the choice and the extent of the clients' belief rest with them.

4. Earning the clients' confidence. The readers emphasize that the success of the reading relies to a large extent on the clients' truthful cooperation. They state upfront that because of difficulties related to language and communication, it is possible that they would not always convey the exact intended meaning. In such cases, they advise the clients to reinterpret the message in their own words and experience. This plot serves two purposes: the readers provide themselves with an alibi in case their initial reading fails (they divert the blame

from themselves onto the clients); in what follows, the clients strive to fit the readers' generalities to their specific circumstances. Later on, when they reflect on the reading, the clients attribute to the readers a lot more credit than they have actually earned. Evidently, the more active the clients are during the reading, the more successful it is. The skilled readers coax the clients, consciously or unconsciously, to actively search their memory in a way that the reading will seem to them sensible.

5. Use of a gimmick. The use of a gimmick such as a crystal ball, tarot cards, or palm reading fulfills two aims: (1) it lends an atmosphere of specialness to the event and reliability to the reader who supposedly relies on an external "objective" tool, and (2) it acts as a delay device for the readers so that they may plan their next move or statement. While contemplating what to say next, they seem to be thoroughly scrutinizing their ball or their cards or a tiny wrinkle on the palm of their client. In palm reading, for example, in order to detect the specific problem troubling the client as quickly as possible, Hyman suggests telling the clients that since time is limited, they should concentrate on their heart line, which deals with problems of the heart, on the fate line, which indicates their professional aspirations and ambitions, and on the health line. Asking the clients with which line they would rather start is smart, for their reply reveals at once the type of problems they are concerned with.

6. Preparing a list of stock statements. Such statements add volume to the reading as well as fill up the time necessary for the readers to formulate more specific statements. Books, manuals, and internet sites are rich sources for such statements.

7. Eyes wide open. We have seen how correct observations regarding the physical characteristics of the clients' appearance and initial behavior may help the readers. But also, a very general assessment of these characteristics may provide the necessary information for the continuation of the reading. The readers follow closely the impact of their statements on the client and continue their reading accordingly.

8. Attentive ears. During the reading, the clients are eager to tell the readers about their troubles, for they are indeed looking

for a sympathetic ear. In addition, as we have seen in the case of the woman in black (story told by a magician quoted in Hyman's book), at the time they approach the cold readers, many of the clients have already made up their minds or their choices, but they need the approval to go ahead and act on them. The skilled readers allow the clients to speak at will. Hyman tells of a tea-leaf reading in which he participated, and in which the client spoke approximately 75% of the total time. At the end of the reading, she insisted that she never opened her mouth and commended the reader on revealing information that she herself had provided!

9. Impressing the clients that the readers know more than they are revealing. If the readers manage to impress the clients by indicating that they know a lot more than they really do, then the spotting of a single correct item suffices for the clients to believe that from this point onward, the readers know everything. This is also the moment when the clients start opening their hearts.

10. Flattery. Even if at times there are clients who appear to shy away from flattery, they will cherish it anyway, and always. A sentence such as "you are inclined to be suspicious of those who flatter you; it is hard for you to believe that anyone could praise you without an ulterior motive" works wonders on all the clients.

11. Telling the clients what they are eager to hear. In this context, Hyman brings a story about Freud and one of his patients who had been to a fortune-teller long before she was his patient. The fortune-teller predicted that the woman would give birth to twins. Not only did she not have twins, she was never able to bring a child into the world. Notwithstanding the clairvoyant's wrong prediction, every time the woman spoke of her, her face lit up. Freud inferred from this behavior that at the time of the fortune-teller's prediction, his patient yearned for a child. The fortune-teller sensed this and told her what she wished to hear. Hence, fortune-telling is a success when you tell the clients what they mostly or secretly wish for.

Dantalion Jones is one of the pseudonyms of an American author who publishes manuals and handbooks on cold reading and other "supernatural" practices, because according to him, "this is a great way to meet people ... capture their attention and have great fun .... It is also a fun way to earn money". Among other things, he exposes the various tricks and ploys behind these practices and demonstrates how each and every one of us may acquire supernatural powers without much effort. In a handbook he published in 2010, in which he quotes Hyman's principles as well, Jones drafts an example of a stock spiel that he believes ought to be presented to every client during a general reading. He recommends to start with a statement that has a 50% chance of being true (e.g., "you are a very sociable person") and right after it to contradict it with a sentence such as "but sometimes you actually prefer to be alone". This way, the reader will be correct in either case. Here are the stock descriptions:

Intelligence and emotion. You have a very sharp mind. In fact, I sense that you perceived things and think about things on a slightly different level than most people. There are a few things that you will hold very close to the vest because you know some people aren't ready to know these things in the same way you are. You are not inclined to put up with others' nonsense. While you recognize the value of education in your life you value even more the education you've received from life experience.

Money. I don't give investment advice, but I sense that in the area of money you are a risk seeker. Unlike a lot of people, I think you've come to the realization that money doesn't buy happiness, but it does solve a lot of problems. So first and foremost, you've focused your money on problem-solving and then on the fun that it can bring you.

Appearance. As a child you were overly critical of yourself and your appearance, never being satisfied with your hair or your complexion. However, you began to gain more confidence as you grew older. I would say that you've learned a few things about how to deal with the opposite sex and you keep those secrets close to the vest and use them when you need to. A good perfume for you would be ... [use a few brand names].

Career. You are a person who is comfortable making decisions. You work easily in a management or supervisory capacity.

I see someone who can set goals and move in a forthright manner to achieve them. You are not sick a lot and rarely miss work. One of the biggest professional desires is to be given the opportunity to prove what you know you're capable of. It would benefit you to not wait to be given that chance, but instead, choose to act and genuinely prove your professional goals and ambitions.

Health. You have to understand that I don't give medical advice so I can't advise on issues of illness. I comment on health and on the vitality of your body. There is a very good chance that you will outlive your spouse. Because you don't like taking pills or medications you seem to be healthier than others your age.

Why does it work?

Why is cold reading such a success? It would not be fair to simply assume that people are gullible and prone to enticement, and certainly not that they lack the necessary intelligence for a critical evaluation of cold reading, albeit there are such cases as well. Actually, it would not be illogical to claim that in order for the cold reading to succeed, a good measure of intelligence and creativity is required on the part of the clients. From the minute they begin to actively participate in the deciphering of the readers' statements, which are so often contradictory, they become creative problem-solvers who are trying to furnish the statements with meaning and coherence. This task is not unlike an attempt to confer meaning to a work of art, a poem, or even an innocent statement, for all of these are offerings from which we may draw experiences that could be rich and meaningful to us while using our own memories and past experiences.

In other words, the cold reading is successful precisely because it requires from us to employ the same means of understanding that we use in order to find our way through any form of communication. Information or raw knowledge has no meaning in itself – we also need a common context and background, and even then, we have to fill in gaps through analogies and inferences. During the cold reading, both readers and clients make use of the usual processes through which we are accustomed to assigning meaning to the items of information that bombard us unceasingly.

In the 1960s, Joseph Weizenbaum, a German-American professor of computer science from Massachusetts Institute of Technology (MIT) developed a computer program that enabled humans to converse with a computer. The program was named "Doctor", and it was programmed to "talk" in a manner that simulated Carl Rogers.[3] It is relatively easy to imitate this particular therapeutic method since it is based on giving the clients feedback through paraphrasing their own statements. The participants in the experiment, playing the role of patients, typed questions on a typewriter connected to a computer and the computer program printed answers. Following is a typical conversation that took place between a young woman and "Doctor", that is, the computer (the bold font represents the computer):

> Men are all alike.
> **In what way?**
> They're always bugging us about something or other.
> **Can you think of a specific example?**
> Well, my boyfriend made me come here.
> **Your boyfriend made you come here.**
> He says I'm depressed most of the time.
> **I am sorry to hear you are depressed.**
> It's true. I am unhappy.
> **Do you think coming here will help you not to be unhappy?**
> I need some help, that much seems certain.
> **What would it mean to you if you got some help?**
> Perhaps I could learn to get along with my mother.
> **Tell me more about your family.**
> My mother takes care of me.
> **Who else in your family takes care of you?**
> My father.
> **Your father.**
> You are like my father in some ways.
> **What resemblance do you see?**
> You are not very aggressive but I think you don't want me to notice that.
> **What makes you think I am not very aggressive?**

> You don't argue with me.
> **Why do you think I don't argue with you?**
> You are afraid of me.
> **Does it please you to believe I am afraid of you?**
> My father is afraid of everybody.
> **What else comes to mind when you think of your father?**
> Bullies.
> **Does that have anything to do with the fact that your boyfriend made you come here?**

In essence, the computer program was a primitive cold reader. It used stock sentences to conceal its inability to manage a question or a real input, and it used the "patient's" input in order to output the same information and create the impression that it both understands and sympathizes with her. This illusion is so powerful that the "patients", even after having been told that they are facing a simple primitive computer program, could not overcome their stormy emotional reactions, and many of them refused to believe the facts, insisting that behind the typewriter was a sympathetic human being.

In 1967, the American sociologist Harold Garfinkel conducted an experiment in which ten undergraduate students were told that the department of psychiatry was exploring alternative means to psychotherapy in order to offer advice to patients regarding their personal problems. Each participant was seen individually by an experimenter who pretended to be a counselor in training. The participant was asked to discuss the background of a specific problem for which he would seek advice. Then, each participant was asked to present the counselor with a few yes/no questions. The counselor/experimenter was listening to the questions in the adjacent room and responded "yes" or "no" to each question after a standard pause. Without the participants' knowledge, the yes/no answers had been pre-decided according to a table of random numbers that bore no relationship to the specific questions. Notwithstanding, the typical participant was convinced that the counselor understood his problem thoroughly and provided sound advice.

As we pointed out before, statements become meaningful only when readers and participants alike place them in a particular context, using their vast reservoirs of life experiences. Bearing this in mind, the clients are not necessarily acting irrationally when they ascribe meaning to a reading or to a stock spiel. In his book of 1952, the American psychologist Salomon Asch refers to an experiment in which two groups of participants were given the following statement: "I hold it that a little rebellion, now and then, is a good thing and as necessary in the political world as storms are in the physical". The participants were asked to describe its meaning. One group was told that the author of the statement was Thomas Jefferson (which is the truth), and the participants identified with its content and interpreted the word "rebellion" as "agitation", while the other group was told that the statement belonged to Lenin, and they interpreted the word "rebellion" as "revolution".

Many social psychologists claim that the various reactions attest to the irrationality inherent in biased opinions, but Asch suggests that it is possible that the participants responded quite rationally. Considering their background knowledge of Jefferson and Lenin, it was not unreasonable to ascribe different meanings to the same statement when it came from such diametrically opposed figures. If they knew that Jefferson believed in proper governance and peaceful ways, it is within reason that they interpreted the statement accordingly. The same goes for Lenin and his upholding of war and bloodshed.

Finally, we also believe that there is a strong therapeutic element in sessions with cold readers. Some people frequent readers steadily and not just once or every once in a while. The visit itself, the special "spiritual" atmosphere created between the readers and their clients in which the latter is the center of attention, arouse in the clients feelings and sensations which are not present in their daily routines. This, no doubt, makes the clients feel special and unique. In this sense, a session with a reader is not unlike a session with a therapist or counselor.

It is worth noting that individual psychotherapy and psychoanalysis have existed slightly over 100 years, while mystical belief was born with history itself. But as we have seen, cold readers tend to tell their clients what the latter long to hear, saving them the pain and the burden that accompany every meaningful psychotherapy or psychoanalysis when they start touching upon our wounds and our real problems. Both financially as well as time-wise, there is no question which is more appealing. Psychotherapy and psychoanalysis may take a very long time (albeit there are methods whereby treatment may be short and not less effective) and are therefore quite costly. The sessions with the readers may also be quite expensive but do not impose on the clients processes that involve emotional trials and efforts.

How much does it cost?

We have seen so far how cold reading works and why it is so successful. From everything that has been said, we might conclude that cold reading is quite harmless as long as the clients understand what is behind it but still choose to cooperate for the sake of amusement, and the cold reading practices may be quite amusing, indeed. But as we pointed out before, in most cases, people do not tend to seek out cold readers unless they find themselves in indecision, in conflict, in dilemma, or in other emotional difficulties. The president of the Society of American Magicians during the years 1935–1936, Julien J. Proskauer, wrote a book which first came out in 1928 in England titled *Spook Crooks!: Exposing the Secrets of the Prophet-eers Who Conduct Our Wickedest Industry*.[4] The title of the book is an immediate indicator of the author's attitude toward cold reading, and he considered exposing the truth behind its various practices imperative. Proskauer himself was a gifted magician. In addition to being president of the Society of American Magicians, he was a member of many other international clubs and societies of magicians. It is precisely because he was a gifted magician who valued his gift that he was such an ardent foe of the cold readers who presented themselves as real clairvoyants. In his book, he demonstrates how we can swallow fire, read secret messages, walk like ghosts, predict the future, and so on. Proskauer writes,

> Before the following ... revelations were written, considerable thought was given to the subject, and many visits made in New York and vicinity to so-called "spirit mediums". It is not the author's intention in this book to do harm to anyone,

but merely to aid the credulous and superstitious in saving their health and money.

He proceeds to quote letters of complaint from clients who had been swindled by cold readers and lost both their money as well as their faith. In his replies, he exposes the fraudulent methods of these "spirit mediums" and how to obtain a "certificate" for practicing cold reading, a procedure that was associated with the Church back then.

> The cost of becoming a "recognized medium" is very modest. One writes to The National Spiritualistic Alliance of Lake Pleasant, Mass., one of the foremost organizations and makes application for membership. Miss Shirley Whicher is (or was) secretary. Anyone sending one dollar to the association becomes an "Individual Member", and for two dollars this association sends a "medium" or "healer's" certificate. If one desires to start a church there is a charge of five dollars for the "Charter", but ten members are necessary to obtain the "Church Charter".
> ...
> In a pamphlet sold to the "initiated", full instructions on how to fleece the public are given. This booklet is printed as an exposé of spiritualism and is sold as such (possibly to avoid postal authorities preventing its distribution), but in it is given exact instructions how to avoid the police, how to advertise for "clients", how to have believers sign a "receipt" which makes the "minister" immune from arrest as a fortune teller, how to work "donation racket", etc, etc.
> The "donation racket" is used where fees cannot be collected. One medium uses it in this fashion. Before giving a reading, in order to avoid the fortune telling law, he states "I charge you nothing for the reading and advice I will give you. To take care of my time, I request you to simply make a donation to the church". The medium forgets to tell the sitter that he is in most cases the "church".
> ...
> In the booklet on how mediums work, details are given about various practices of fraudulent spiritualists. The author

of the booklet, a man just recently convicted and fined $100, gives complete instructions on how to read messages written by believers. While the method he gives differs from ones explained by me in many articles, the same underlying principle is used, that of substituting blank paper for the paper on which the message is written.

Therefore, let me tell you to never write anything on paper in a medium's meeting. No matter how innocent the moves of the medium may be, trickery is being used to find out your question. And the answer you get is just so much nonsense.

The medium's instruction book, for one can call it nothing else, tells how to give "psychological readings" and states "it all depends on the medium's ability to handle the sitter and to repeat a stock spiel". The word spiel to the initiated means "talk". The jargon of the author of the booklet is the jargon of the show business.

...

Unbelievable as it may be, Harry Houdini[5] had in his possessions at his death hundreds of "certificates of Ordination" issued to uneducated, ignorant people who become "ministers" almost for the asking. Some of these certificates were issued by the National Spiritualistic Alliance and others by the National Spiritualistic Association of Washington, D.C.

Proskauer cites examples of cold readers whom he visited accompanied by friends, who were erroneous in their readings of the specifications of his friends because they did not volunteer any information without being unaware of it. He concludes this chapter as follows:

In closing this chapter, as further proof that "gross fraud" is prevalent among spirit mediums I want to reproduce here (in part) a letter to Harry Houdini from the late Dr. A. M. Wilson of Kansas City, Editor and Publisher of *The Sphinx* for more than a score of years. *The Sphinx*, privately circulated magazine for magicians and official organ of the Society of American Magicians, in Dr. Wilson's regime ran story after story exposing frauds of mediums, and today under the editorship of John Mulholland, refuses all advertising of any apparatus that may be used by fake spirit mediums. The letter:

1007 Main St.,
Kansas City, Mo.

Dear Houdini:

For almost 61 years I have been witnessing and investigating Spiritualism as propagated by mediums through their so-called communications with the dead. Up to this time, I have never met a medium, celebrated or obscure, who was not a gross fraud, nor seen a manifestation that was not trickery and that could not be duplicated by any expert magician.

The thing that first aroused my suspicions and disbeliefs and started me thinking and investigating was why could not the dear departed communicate direct with their relatives and friends? Why talk, rap, write or materialize through a medium, the majority of whom are ignorant men and women, although shrewd and cunning?

I have never met a medium who was not a fraud or seen a materialization of any kind that was not fraudulent.

(signed) A. M. WILSON, M.D.

Almost 100 years have passed since the writing of these lines, and despite the vast changes that have occurred in the (Western) world and society, nothing has changed in the area of cold reading, except for the fees we have to pay for it, of course. Issue no. 169 of the Israeli magazine (in Hebrew) *Lady Globes* from October 2012 dedicates 50% of its content to articles, interviews, and essays on cold readers and their clients, under the general title "Beyond the Rational". In one of these articles, titled "The Black Market", the author states that

> the cold readers market is a multi-million Israeli Shekel market in which readers charge between IS 1000 and 2000 (around 300 to 600 US Dollars) for a first meeting that lasts between half an hour to one hour. For longer sessions, weekly sessions, and assessments of business moves the charge is much

higher. One central figure in the cold reading market charges IS3000 [approx. $1000], and prominent business men and women pay her the fees once they have gotten acquainted with her magical powers.

One of the cold readers brags: "The future of the Israeli economy does not really depend on the business people, but on the spiritual readers who tell them what to do. Funny? Maybe, but this is the reality". Well, considering everything we have shown in this chapter, not only do we not find this very funny, we find it quite alarming.

But the cost paid by the clients is not confined to money alone. It can also be psychological, emotional, social, and quite detrimental to one's future. Let us look at an artistic example: Woody Allen's film (2010) *You Will Meet a Tall Dark Stranger* is a film that deals, among other things, with decision-making based on fortune-telling and contacting the spirits of the dead. Helena, an older woman whose husband Alfie has abandoned her in the search for his long-lost youth, does not take a step without consulting first with her fortune-teller, Cristal, much to the dismay of her daughter Sally, and especially her son-in-law Roy who does not miss an opportunity to tell her that she's throwing her money in vain. In her desperate need to cope with her new situation, Helena meets Jonathan, an older, chubby, bald widower (the answer to the "tall dark stranger" Cristal predicts!), who at first hesitates to commit to her since he is still loyal to his dead wife, Clair. Only after he receives his dead wife's blessing during a séance is he willing to commit to his relationship with Helena.

At the beginning of the film, Allen goes back to Sally's and Roy's courtship when they were still very much in love. Lying idly on the grass in a park, Allen has Roy fondly reciting to Sally "The Red Wheelbarrow", a short poem by the American Imagist poet William Carlos Williams, in which he states that "so much depends on a red wheelbarrow".

What purpose does this intertextuality serve? It seems that Allen draws a parallel between the belief in fortune-tellers and the experience we undergo in the encounter with a work of art, in this case, a poem and a film. In his poem, Williams refers us to a random, concrete image and tells us that a lot depends on it. We are expected to accept this statement as a truthful statement.

This acceptance, or if you may, this faith, enables us to draw pleasure and satisfaction from the poet's image, and this pleasure and satisfaction are the "so much" that both the poet and Allen refer to.

This cognitive position of the fiction consumer was termed by the English Romantic poet Samuel Taylor Coleridge "willing suspension of disbelief". The readers or spectators are well aware of the fact that they are witnessing a fictitious narrative, but the total experience provoked/evoked by this narrative depends on a temporary oversight or neglect of this awareness. It seems that Allen suggests here that the total experience of organizing one's life according to the predictions and premonitions of fortune-tellers – and their partial or full success – depends on our will to suspend our awareness of the fact that it is fiction we are dealing with. In that, cold reading is a sort of fiction that relies on willing suspension of disbelief (and, as we have seen, its suppliers are quite artful), just as the extent of our enjoyment from a work of art relies on the extent of our willing suspension of disbelief.

Allen shows us that the belief in cold reading is all nice and well, so long as it remains in the realm of art or amusement. In one of the scenes, Sally tries to persuade Roy (who hates Cristal and his mother-in-law's visits with her) that her mother's sessions with Cristal are better than taking pills. But when Sally asks her mother for a loan in order to fulfill her dream and open an art gallery of her own and her mother turns her down because "Cristal says it's not the right time", Sally loses her temper completely and starts cursing and calling them names, both Cristal ("fraud") and her mother ("stupid idiot", "imbecile", and so on). Her efforts to make her mother see that she's throwing her money on a fraud who takes advantage of her gullibility are not successful. To what extent is the mother's ending a happy one is a question subjected to our "cold reading" – she wins a new love because she does not budge an inch from her blind faith in Cristal's predictions and is wholly invested in them, but the price she pays is double: parting with a fortune that could have benefited her daughter as well as the deterioration of her relationship with her.

At this point, we would like to share with you a personal story experienced by Marianna, and therefore, it will be narrated in first person.

Some years ago, around my birthday, my husband Gershon's son and his daughter-in-law arrived at our family Friday night dinner, all wired up from what had transpired that same morning. They proceeded to tell us that following some friend's advice, they went to see a tarot reader, whom I shall also call "Cristal"[6] (and not by her real name, of course), and that she had told them the most amazing facts about their lives, their problems, and their first-born son. They added that all the reader had asked to know before the meeting with her was their dates of birth and their first names.

When we tried to intervene in the conversation and explain how cold reading works, our children refused to hear any critique or disbelief from us, bombarding us with one example after another, such as "how do you explain that she knew that our son is stubborn, that he has problems falling asleep at night, that he resembles his grandfather, and that his grandfather is a well-known, respected, figure?" and so on. At long last we arrived at a compromise whereby I agreed to meet with Cristal myself. Our children insisted that this should be their gift for my birthday. My agreement was conditioned upon remaining completely silent during the visit, allowing Cristal the opportunity to "read" my situation, my character, my future, and so on, without any intervention on my part. I called Cristal and left my birthdate and my first name with her.

When I arrived at the meeting, Cristal led me into a room, quite spacious but packed with objects related to the mystical world. She sat down cross-legged on a wide carpet spread in the middle of the room and invited me to join her. I did as she requested, whereupon she proceeded, while carefully examining her cards, to state that I was an important person in the world of finance. To quote her precisely, "You're working with something ... something that has to do with a lot of money, a lot of responsibility for budgets, finances, something related to that ...". Now, I have never worked in anything remotely financial nor have I ever been seriously interested in the financial world, other than in my own personal expenditures and revenues. My interests and passions have always revolved, and still do, around literature, poetry, translation (which had also been my subjects of studies), cinema and art in general, and at the time of the reading,

I was still working at the Hebrew University as Advisor to New and Visiting Faculty, dealing with academic subjects that did not necessitate any financial work from me. At this point, I will put the cart before the horse and state that when I got back home, I googled my first name and there it was, on the Hebrew University site, the information pertaining to a committee on gender issues that I had initiated. My name appeared next to the financial/budgetary activity related to the work of the committee, and so I assumed that Cristal had drawn her assumptions from there. I remained true to my condition to stay still and silent (which is quite hard to do in this kind of dynamics, for psychologically speaking, we want the reading to succeed!). I refrained from confirming or denying Cristal's statements. Not getting any feedback from me, she continued along the same lines, but I started noticing signs of tribulations as well as a total lack of direction. Indeed, from that point onward she repeatedly accused me in a growing irritated voice that I am not cooperating and that she cannot do her job without any help from me! When I responded that I came to her so that *she* could tell me something that I do not know about myself and illuminate my life in a different light, she ruled that I was her first client to behave like that and that she did not understand why I had come to see her if I'm not interested in the reading. When she finally gave up on me, without any request from me, and probably to leave some impression on me, she started talking about my husband, releasing true statements about him: that he is a psychologist, that he is older than me, "an important man", and "an important executive" (at that time Gershon was president of the Open University in Israel). All of the information could have been easily drawn from Gershon's numerous internet entries. Evidently, the fact that she displayed a lot more familiarity with Gershon's as opposed to my own specifications, reinforced my assumption that she had dug up the information from the internet and perhaps from other sources too, as cold readers do.

Thus passed a whole hour of awkwardness and embarrassment, at the end of which Cristal said to me, "Isn't there anything you wish to ask me"? I replied positively and asked her if I would ever publish a poetry book (in my youth I had the ambition to become a poet). "NO"! she resolved decisively, with a grain of gloat in her voice. Well, I already knew the answer to this question, for I can never have a book I do not intend to write, but I was convinced that Cristal acted out to retaliate to my disobedience and refusal to cooperate with her. And, what would have happened had Cristal made such a prediction to a young woman, who unlike me, had not yet parted with her dream and had taken her words at face value? Might she not have despaired and abandoned any serious attempt to materialize her passion? What good is making any effort at all if Cristal has already pronounced the verdict? But such a scenario is not very likely, albeit possible, since as we have repeatedly pointed out in this chapter, as a rule, that the clients are more than cooperative and volunteer a lot of information in return for which the readers endow them with statements and predictions that correspond to their hopes and desires.

I left the encounter with Cristal feeling profoundly sad. I thought I was feeling this way because I would have to let down the kids who had spent IS500 on such a futile gift. I could not help thinking that if a regular day's work is eight hours and Cristal receives – let us say – six persons per day and rests a while in between readings, she earns IS3,000 per day, which totals IS75,000 per month (25 days of work)! When I arrived home and shared my experience with Gershon, his reaction was, "You got today a good dose of the two things you hate most in the world – stupidity and dishonesty, no wonder you're sad"!

Anyone can conduct this experiment. It is possible, though it requires some effort, to refrain from any comments and cooperation with the cold reader during the meeting. Another possibility, which could prove quite amusing, is to pose as a person in a situation opposed to your real one and see what such behavior may produce. If you are generally satisfied with your life, you could dress up in rags, appear morose and depressed, and steer the conversation accordingly. We promise that the readers will slide into the trap provided you play your role right. But, we will say it again, unfortunately, as a rule, people turn to cold readers when they are truly unhappy or lost.

To end this chapter, we propose one simple, and especially funny, solution to the constant search for a logical explanation to cold readers' superpowers. Participants in cold readings tend to, like our kids, wonder how it is possible to logically explain a phenomenon that is clearly illogical. The most readily available answer is that if a phenomenon does not have a logical explanation, then it stands to reason that it is related to the readers' superpowers. Amos Tversky, the well-known Israeli psychologist, was once asked how he explained the fact that Uri Geller can drive a car blindfolded. "He simply reads the road's mind", replied Tversky complacently.

Notes

1 See, for example, in the bibliography of Paul Huson's book, *Mystical Origins of the Tarot: From Ancient Use to Modern Usage*.
2 The interview may be viewed on YouTube under *Orson Wells and Cold Reading*, alongside more amusing filmstrips on cold reading.
3 Carl Rogers (1902–1987) was an American psychologist, among the founders of the "humanistic approach" in psychology, father of the "person/client-centered therapy". Rogers believed that the main human motivation is the drive for self-fulfillment, and that many psychological problems are rooted in the gap that exists between "the real self" and "the ideal self". He believed that this incongruity can be prevented through education and unconditional acceptance of the individual and her/his feelings. Similarly, the clinical psychologist/therapist should be a supportive, warm, sympathetic, guiding figure, and not necessarily an authoritative one.
4 See www.survivalafterdeath.info/articles/proskauer/medium.
5 The famous illusionist and stunt performer (1874–1926).
6 Cristal's name in Allen's film alludes, of course, to the crystal ball that many readers use.

Bibliography

Asch, S.E. (1952). *Social Psychology*. Englewood Cliffs, NJ: Prentice-Hall Inc.
Forer, B.R. (1949). The fallacy of personal validation: A classroom demonstration of gullibility. *Journal of Abnormal and Social Psychology*, 44, 118–123.
Garfinkel, H. (1967). *Studies in Ethnomethodology*. Englewood Cliffs, NJ: Prentice-Hall.
Gilboa, G. (1995). *A Complete Tarot Course* (in Hebrew). Hod Hasharon, Israel: Astrolog.

Huson, P. (2004). *Mystical Origins of the Tarot*. Rochester, VT: Destiny Books.

Hyman, R. (1989). *The Elusive Quarry: A Scientific Appraisal of Psychical Research*. Buffalo, NY: Prometheus Books.

Jones, D. (2010). *The Handbook of Psychic Cold Reading*. ISBN: 1449906222.

Lady Globes (October 2012, in Hebrew). No. 169.

Proskauer, J.J. (1928). *Spook Crooks! Exposing the Secrets of the Prophet-eers Who Conduct Our Wickedest Industry*. London, UK: Selwyn & Blount.

Sundberg, N.D. (1955). The acceptability of "fake" versus "bona fide" personality test interpretation. *Journal of Abnormal and Social Psychology*, 50, 145–147.

Weizenbaum, J. (1976). *Computer Power and Human Reason: From Judgment to Calculation*. Oxford, UK: W.H. Freeman & co.

Websites mentioned

www.survivalafterdeath.info/articles/proskauer/medium
http://sharp-thinking.com/2011
www.physics.smu.edu/pseudo/cold
www.deceptionary.com/aboutreading.html

2

"They love you and you know that"[1]
Astrology

> But what I understood to be your anticipation for the wisdom of the stars, and the evil spirits that have come or may come to pass – banish them from your heart and wash your mind off of them like one washes dirty clothes from their dirt, as there is neither truth nor fact in them.
>
> **Maimonides** (from *Epistle to Yemen*)

An overview of astrology

"Not the astrologers have deceived us when they assured us that there was no immediate threat pending from the gulf area. The stars had deceived them, even though they won't admit it". This is a quote, uttered by an astrologer, from an Israeli daily newspaper (*Ha'aretz*) in February 1991, following the prediction of most astrologers that a war was not imminent in the Persian Gulf during that period. Three facts are clear in this statement which could not be more ironic: (1) the astrologers are wrong, (2) the astrologers are not taking responsibility for their mistake, and (3) the astrologers cannot rely on the stars. These three facts are linked to each other for, in the absence of any logical explanation regarding the astrologers' ability to foresee the future, it is also impossible to explain why they were wrong, and so, *not* they are at fault but the stars themselves. Alas, if they cannot rely on the stars, what *can* they rely on? This chapter is an attempt to show how astrology and other similar practices work, all of which are based on an identical psychological mechanism of interaction between the suppliers and their clients.

The practice of astrology rests on the belief that there is a connection between our situation, our actions, and our characteristics on earth and the position of the other planets in the universe. Astrology claims not only to be able to describe our situation in the present but also to be able to predict our future. As far as astrologers are concerned, astrology may be applied to all our venues of life and even to supposed past reincarnations.

As Jim Tester states in the introduction to his book, *A History of Western Astrology*, "star-gazing is ... far older than philosophy, and older than history ...". Astrology – the combination of star-gazing and philosophy – was born most probably in Mesopotamia toward the end of the second millennium BC. At its outset and for many years thereafter, it served less of private use and mainly to prophesize events of public importance which impacted the well-being of the general public. It is believed that Babylonian astrology started pervading the Western culture during the Hellenistic period at the beginning of the fourth century BC. It was Berossus of Kos who introduced astrology to Greece while the Greek philosophers prepared the ground for its acceptance. They took star-gazing and philosophy, added geometry and rational thought to it, and produced the art of astrology. Indeed, the first to use and develop astrology were the scholars, particularly the Stoics. In due course, the Greeks also developed personal astrology, that is, the horoscope (*hora* – hour, *skopos* – observation), which was based on the chart of the stars at the time of birth. Notwithstanding, astrology became popular in Greece only in the second century AD, when the Hellenistic philosopher Ptolemy wrote the *Tetrabiblos* [*The Four Books*], which for many centuries was considered to be the most influential book of astrology. Ptolemy was also the father of the geocentric concept in astronomy, according to which the earth is the center of the universe.

In the Middle Ages, astrology met with great opposition, including from the Christian Church, which stemmed mainly from its deterministic philosophy, that is, that everything is predetermined, and therefore, human beings are not accountable for their acts.

As mentioned above, astrology penetrated most cultures around the world; hence, various traditions have developed: Babylonian, Hellenistic, Indian, astrology of the Middle Ages and the Renaissance, modern Western astrology, Chinese astrology, and Kabbalistic astrology.

Astrology and astronomy walked hand in hand until the Middle Ages. But in the new era, astrology was brushed aside with other practices based on mysticism and faith alone and not on the tenets of science. While the science of astronomy has taught us much about the universe, Western astrology is firmly linked with the cosmologic view that indeed believes in the earth-centered universe. The Copernican revolution in the sixteenth century and the modern developments in astronomy and in classical mechanics overthrew this belief, but oddly enough, the fundamentals of astrology have not developed nor changed.

Modern Western astrology is based on astrological maps, calculated for a specific time, mostly our time of birth. The maps are analyzed according to the alignment of the stars, the angles between them, and their position. The astrologic calculations involved in placing the stars in specific times use matrices prepared in advance and necessitate simple arithmetic and geometry.

Had the astrologers and their clients accepted astrology as a kind of "art", as it is conceived by Tester, it would not have been necessary to mobilize critical thinking in order to analyze it. But because astrologers make objective, measurable assertions, which fill the various writings on the topic, and because this practice is so popular, it is imperative that we ask: Do their claims have any foundations? Can they be refuted? Let us examine what science has had to say about it.

Astrology and science

In 1975, 186 leading scientists, among whom were notable astronomers and 18 Nobel Prize winners, signed the following petition published in the American journal *The Humanist*, a journal of critical thought and social awareness.

Scientists in a variety of fields have become concerned about the increased acceptance of astrology in many parts of the world. We, the undersigned – astronomers, astrophysicists, and scientists in other fields – wish to caution the public against the unquestioning acceptance of the predictions and advice given privately and publicly by astrologers. Those who wish to believe in astrology should realize that there is no scientific foundation for its tenets.

In ancient times people believed in the predictions and advice of astrologers because astrology was part and parcel of their magical world view. They looked upon celestial objects as abodes or omens of the gods and, thus, intimately connected with events here on earth; they had no concept of the vast distances from the earth to the planets and stars. Now that these distances can and have been calculated, we can see how infinitesimally small are the gravitational and other effects produced by the distant planets and the far more distant stars. It is simply a mistake to imagine that the forces exerted by stars and planets at the moment of birth can in any way shape our futures. Neither is it true that the position of distant heavenly bodies make certain days or periods more favorable to particular kinds of action, or that the sign under which one was born determines one's compatibility or incompatibility with other people.

Why do people believe in astrology? In these uncertain times many long for the comfort of having guidance in making decisions. They would like to believe in a destiny predetermined by astral forces beyond their control. However, we must all face the world, and we must realize that our futures lie in ourselves, and not in the stars.

One would imagine, in this day of widespread enlightenment and education, that it would be unnecessary to debunk beliefs based on magic and superstition. Yet, acceptance of astrology pervades modern society. We are especially disturbed by the continued uncritical dissemination of astrological charts, forecasts, and horoscopes by the media and by otherwise reputable newspapers, magazines, and book publishers. This can only contribute to the growth of irrationalism and obscurantism. We believe that the time has come to challenge directly, and forcefully, the pretentious claims of astrological charlatans.

It should be apparent that those individuals who continue to have faith in astrology do so in spite of the fact that there is <u>no verified scientific basis</u> for their beliefs, and indeed that there is strong evidence to the contrary.

Forty-two years have passed since the publication of this petition, but nothing has changed. Astrology continues to star, quite equivocally, in magazines, newspapers, and, of course, in electronic media. In truth, its most astonishing aspect, as Tester points out, is

> that self-styled ancient art is today very much as the Greeks formed it. It was they who took the star-gazing and its magic and mumbo-jumbo and added philosophy, added geometry and rational thought about themselves and their universe, and produced the art of astrology.

The French Michel Gauquelin, born in 1928, who earned a BA degree in Statistics and Psychology from the Sorbonne University, was the most important researcher of astrology in the modern era. From an early age, he was fascinated with stars and astrology, and while still a child, he read about 100 books on the topic and learned how to design charts. In his fascination and continuous pursuit of astrology, he did not give up the hope of finding scientific validity for his claims. Gauquelin devoted 40 years of his life to research on astrology and published his findings in books and numerous articles, in collaboration with his first wife, Francoise. But despite his passion and dedication, he was unsuccessful in convincing serious scientists of his claims. As far as the horoscope goes, he himself concluded, in an article published in 1982 in *The Skeptical Inquirer*, after having gathered half a million birthdates from a variety of people, that there is no correlation between character traits of the subjects and the signs under which they were born. In 1991, Gauquelin sank into depression and committed suicide. In an obituary Francoise wrote, she stressed that he was a thorough, conscientious researcher and that the numerous battles he had to fight with his opponents wore him down. Francoise, no doubt, sympathized with her husband in whose efforts she had participated. But wouldn't we, as critical thinkers, want to ask why Gauquelin was so alone in his claims and so criticized by scientists who tried to replicate his findings? To answer this question, we will take a close look at Gauquelin's most well-known finding, the **Mars effect**. Since we do not wish to burden the readers with the detailed statistical calculations neither in Gauquelin's work nor in the studies that ensued, we will concentrate mainly on the main "theoretical" claim and its refutation, as reflected in the essay published by Paul Kurtz and his colleagues in 1997, who concluded that there is insufficient evidence for the Mars effect, and that this effect may be attributed to "Gauquelin's selective bias in either discarding or adding data post hoc".

Michel and Francoise Gauquelin claimed that there is a correlation between the position of the planets in the universe at the exact time of birth and personality traits and professional achievements. For example, that there is a correlation between Jupiter and military men, Saturn and scientists, Mars and accomplished athletes, and so on. They claimed to have found a statistically significant correlation between the position of the planet Mars and the exact times and places of the birth of sports champions.

Researchers have spent decades patiently sifting through the claims of the so-called evidence adduced to support the Mars effect. But as Kurtz and his colleagues show, the effect was never fully replicated. They conclude that if the Mars effect had been real, it should have been confirmed by other independent researchers, and that tests conducted in the US and France have been unable to replicate it. So, it must be that the effect had been based upon Gauquelin's bias:

> There are several rather compelling indications that this is so. His reactions to the U.S. test showed his efforts to redefine eminence, in full knowledge of the results, after the test was over. An examination of his files showed that he was doing the same thing privately with his own data. He also tried to influence the French [committee] test in various ways by adding, deleting and changing records. We have adduced evidence that both in the 1960s and in the 1970s he discarded data that he thought unreliable. Perhaps some

of this evidence could have been discovered 20 years ago or more, if scientists at that time had focused less on astronomy and more on Gauquelin's procedures in data collection. In other words, the key witness who claimed a remarkable effect turns out to be unreliable, and we must return a verdict of "not proven".

We also find the fact that Gauquelin ordered to burn all of his data after his death quite dubious.

But the efforts to investigate astrology through scientific tools did not start and die with Gauquelin. In 1981 a group of scientists published an appeal that was sent to thousands of students around the world. The scientists challenged the students to provide some sort of empirical proof of the validity of the zodiac signs. They received a handful of answers, and not one of them provided any such new evidence. Other attempts followed, but not a single study showed any evidence of the connection between the characteristics attributed to each sign and those belonging to people born under them. Quite the contrary, there is evidence that refutes any such connection.

In 1983, the Canadian scholars Betty Surenton and Catherine Fichter conducted a research that focused on the predictions of various astrological signs. They asked 366 students to check their daily and monthly horoscopes distributed by two different astrologers. When the signs above the predictions were being exposed, the students found the prediction matching, but when the signs were covered, they found the predictions aimed for the other signs equally matching. The results show that the prior knowledge is the crucial factor leading to the sensation of matching. This is an example of the "confirmation bias" phenomenon, on which we will elaborate later on. At this stage, we will simply point out that numerous studies in social psychology have demonstrated our tendency to confirm our prior expectations – in other words, to find confirmation of our prior opinions, assumptions, hypothesis, and wishful thinking. Indeed, who would not marvel at a most promising opening statement such as "you know you are loved"?

The British-German psychologist Hans Eysenck, one of the most well-known and most cited scholars in the fields of intelligence and personality, attempted in most of his studies on many diverse topics to quantify various facets in the human personality such as humor, sexual behavior, and intelligence. Among his topics of interest were also astrology, graphology, and extrasensory perception.

In 1971 (20 years before Gauquelin's death), the British astrologer Jeff Mayo sent Eysenck a study he had conducted on 1,795 subjects, in which he compared their measure of extraversion (as indicated by them in a questionnaire drafted by Mayo) with the sign under which they were born. The results showed a pattern in total accordance with astrology. Eysenck was intrigued and made his Personality Inventory (his own questionnaire) available to Mayo for further tests. The outcome was a paper by Mayo, White and Eysenck (1978) detailing Eysenck's results for 2,324 subjects, which, again, yielded a pattern in agreement with astrology. The journal of astrology *Phenomena* declared this as "the most important development for astrology in this century". But later on, Eysenck realized that the examinees in the experiments were devout believers of astrology, as most of them had been selected from Mayo's students and clients. Therefore, it was safe to assume that they were familiar with the characteristics attributed to their signs. Indeed, the effect disappeared when people unfamiliar with sun signs were tested. In other words, the subjects were already biased toward astrology. In 1982, Eysenck published a book (with David Nias) describing a long survey that examined scientific evidence for astrology, *Astrology: Science or Superstition?* They covered astrological principles, sun signs, marriage, illness, suicide, appearance, season of birth, terrestrial and solar cycles, radio propagation, earthquakes, and lunar effects. Eysenck and Nias concluded (as did a year later Surenton and Fichter) that much of the acceptance of astrological readings was explained by the Barnum effect. In his own words, "If the most basic tenets of astrology are true, they should be detectable in their own right .... If astrology is true, it must pass that kind of test". Eysenck wrote several papers on research methods in astrology, became one of the most cited psychologists, and inspired future researchers of astrology.

We may learn from all this that not the birthdate is what affects our character traits. It is our expectation to be of a certain character that influences our self-perception and even our behavior (we will touch upon this subject in Chapter 5).

Against these conclusions, astrologers claim that they are based on the study of the connections between the astrological sun sign under which we are born and our character traits, and that only on the basis of a full birth chart, the exact date and time of birth, can we comprehend the full extent of the power of astrology. Evidently, this claim constitutes an immediate nullification of the entire horoscope industry, which, as we know, does not take into account the exact date of birth of each and every one of us. Let us examine an example of research that tested "the full extent of the power of astrology".

In 1985, Shawn Carlson published in the most prestigious journal *Nature* what was regarded the most comprehensive test of astrologers' abilities to extract information about their clients from the apparent positions of celestial objects as seen from the places and times of their clients' births. Carlson's study involved 28 astrologers who were held in high esteem by their peers and were fully involved in outlining the study and the approval of its protocol. The study involved two tests. In the first one, astrological charts were given to 83 participants based on their exact birth details. Each participant was given three personality descriptions, one intended for him and the two others intended for other participants. Only in 28 of the 83 cases did the participants choose the chart intended for them, just as it would have happened had they chosen one of the three personality descriptions blindfolded. In the second test, 116 participants filled out the California Psychological Inventory (CPI), a standard and well-accepted personality test, in which they supplied their birthdates. Each astrologer received a personality description of three participants drafted from the questionnaire they had filled out, as well as the birthdate of *one* of the three. Their task was to determine which one of the three personality descriptions matches the birthdate. Only in 40 of the 116 cases did the astrologers ascribe the personality description to the birthdate correctly. Again, a result no better than this would have been obtained by chance. Once again, the astrological hypothesis was refuted. More similar tests were conducted over the years and obtained identical results.

As we have seen, the knowledge that we have accumulated from controlled tests (and we will elaborate later on, on what a controlled test is) demonstrates unequivocally that there is absolutely no empirical validity to the claim that from observing the stars in the universe there is anything to be learned about our personality and history, and most certainly not our future.

Note

1 Thus begins the daily horoscope of the sign Aries of August 30, 2017, on www.astrology.com.

Bibliography

Carlson, S. (1985). A double-blind test of astrology. *Nature, 318,* 419–425.

Eysenck, H.J., & Nias, D.K.B. (1984). *Astrology: Science or Superstition?* Harmondsworth, UK: Penguin Books.

Gauquelin, Z. (1982). Zodiac and personality: An empirical study. *Skeptical Inquirer, 6*(3), 57.

Kurtz, P., Nienhuys, J.W., & Sandhu, R. (1997). Is the Mars effect genuine? *Journal of Scientific Exploration, 11,* 19–39.

Mayo, J., White, O., & Eysenck, H.J. (1978). An empirical study of the relation between astrological factors and personality. *The Journal of Social Psychology, 105,* 229–236.

Sunerton, B., & Fichter, C.S. (1983). *Scientific Study of Astrology: A Laboratory Manual for the Institutional Research Committee.* Montreal, QC: Dawson College.

Tester, S.J. (1987). *A History of Western Astrology.* Suffolk, UK: St. Edmundsbury Press.

Websites mentioned

http://sharp-thinking.com/2011
www.astrology-and-science.com
www.planetos.info

3

Show me your handwriting and I'll tell you who you are
Graphology

> Most people in Israel, especially those who express an interest in the various branches of graphology, were pleased to find out how most graphologists who have examined Mordechai Vanunu's signature have managed to establish so succinctly his character and his biography just by examining his signature. It was especially wonderful to see how most graphologists wrote that albeit the fact that they knew Vanunu and of him, they could immediately see from his signature that he was single, probably childless, that he spent some time in Australia, and also, that at present, he is incarcerated in Israel.

This amusing paragraph appeared in the context of the Vanunu spying affair[1] in *Davar Aher* (the satirical section of the newspaper *Davar*, which disappeared from the market some years ago), on November 19, 1987. Another funny announcement placed in the same issue stated: "Atid [in Hebrew - future] Zukunpath, graphologist, will determine from your biography and inclinations with the utmost precision, the shape of your handwriting"! As amusing as these statements may be, we believe that it is worth examining seriously the graphologists' claims to be able to diagnose character traits according to people's handwriting, for, as we will see later on, graphology is a common popular tool used by many for various purposes, including screening and classifying personnel in various occupational sectors.

Scott Lilienfeld and his colleagues refer in their book to an article that appeared in the *Los Angeles Times* in 2008 during the presidential campaigns of Barack Obama versus John McCain. The article maintained that McCain's tendency to sign his name with letters slanted in opposite directions attests to his independent nonconformist character, while his opponent's tendency to shape his letters smoothly is evidence of his flexibility. Many other examples of the graphologists' claim that handwriting reflects character traits as well as human conditions are brought in Bar-Hillel and Ben-Shakhar's essay. Do you know, for instance, that people whose strokes of pen end in marked sharpness have sadistic inclinations? That those who end their signature in a line crossing the first letter of their name have suicidal tendencies? That women may save unnecessary medical examinations and expenses when the letter "g" (in Hebrew ג) starts swelling in their writing, for this is sure evidence of their being pregnant? In this chapter, we will try to see what lies behind all these arguments and to what extent their scientific claims are valid.

Science and Pseudo science

Since the current chapter, as well as the one following it (dealing with the polygraph), discusses practices based on pseudo-science, we would like to pause for a moment and shed some light on the differences between real science and pseudo-science. And since there is no standard way to define science, in our context, we will refer solely to the principles of experimental science. To this end, we have adopted the following five principles.[2]

Experimental science deals with questions that *are essentially solvable*. In that, scientists pose questions which may be answered through accessible empirical techniques, according to technological developments and accumulated knowledge. Experimental scientists do not address questions which are not essentially solvable. Questions such as "Is planet earth the center of the universe"? or "Will three-year-olds who are exposed to linguistic stimuli learn to read and write faster than other children"? are scientific questions which might be answered through systematic methodical observations. On the other hand, questions such as "Is the human being fundamentally good or bad"?, "What is the meaning of life"? or "Does the universe have unity and purpose"? are not scientific questions in the sense that we are discussing science, and no laboratory will ever provide answers for them. From this, we may learn that science is limited to the physical world, including human cognition, and does not presume to tackle all existing phenomena or cultural products and constructions.

Scientists do not aspire to provide perfect knowledge regarding our world. In truth, science's unique potency comes not from its processes being flawless but from its ability to provide ways to eliminate mistakes and misconceptions from our accumulated knowledge. But pseudo-science does not confine itself in any way and will add to its wagon any problem or issue.

In this context, it is important to distinguish between "science" and "truth". To say that a specific theory is scientific does not necessarily mean that it is true or right, for there have been and always will be incorrect scientific theories. Indeed, a good scientific theory is tested, among other things, through *refutation*. And, to say that a theory is not scientific does not necessarily mean that it is incorrect or false. Science constitutes a method through which we may learn about the truth, but there are other means that share the same purpose, as logic, for example. Albeit the differences of opinion among philosophers of logic, they will all agree on the validity of logic, as well as on the fact that it might be exposed through means unrelated to experimental science.

The second principle we have adopted is *the use of systematic empirical evidence and reliance on theories that can be tested*. But empirical evidence in itself is not enough. We can record all the activities we perform daily and hourly and not learn from it a single solitary thing. Scientific observations must be systematic, in that they must be conducted so that they will lead to results that may shed light on the theory that is being tested. One of the characteristics of systematic observation is *control*. For example, when the efficiency of a new drug is being tested, it is necessary to compare the people who have received the drug with people who have not. When such a comparison is being examined, rigorous control is required, in that both groups of examinees must be identical in all their significant characteristics, outside the fact that one has been given the drug and the other has not. In particular, both groups have to be sampled from the same population and tested through identical conditions. In addition, it is paramount to ensure that the group that has not been given the drug (the control group) is not aware of it, for the very knowledge may act as an influential factor. Therefore, in such tests it is customary to give the control group a placebo drug.[3] However, pseudo-science does not rely on any controlled experiments nor does it employ systematic observations.

The third important principle of experimental science is *replicability*. In that, we expect the results obtained in a specific experiment to be obtained also in further ones relying on the same methodology. Scientific observations, as a rule, are motivated by a certain theory, and they are constructed in a way that will permit the results to either support or refute the theory. Indeed, as we have pointed out, science also advances through the refutation of theories. But pseudo-science is totally devoid of any theoretical basis, nor does it rely on any irrefutable theories, and it searches typically only for supportive evidence. Since we may find supportive evidence for almost any claim in the world, relying uniquely on them when we test a hypothesis is an unequivocally inefficient strategy and a prescription for perpetuating errors.

The fourth characteristic of true science is *peer reviewing* of the experiments and their results, and their accessibility to the scientific community at large through publication. Knowledge possessed by one individual or another, immune to criticism from peers and other experts, is not considered scientific. We do not mean to pretend that science itself is immune to mistakes, but criticism from peers and publication enable the rectification of errors and misconceptions in the long run. While the process of peer-reviewing is not flawless, it is still the most efficient mechanism for rectifying scientific mistakes and wrong assumptions. It also aids researchers to identify erroneous thought, methodology, and means of analyzing findings. The claims relying on pseudo-science are not in the least exposed to such scrutiny. This is also a sure path for perpetuation errors.

The fifth and final principle we have adopted to describe experimental science is *connectivity* among the various scientific fields. For example, it is not possible to develop a theory in biology that will contradict the existing laws of physics. But pseudo-science advances (or not) in complete disregard for the knowledge accumulated in other fields. A good example of this may be the claim for the existence of extrasensory perception that contradicts basic physical laws.

Let us resume the subject of graphology now, and examine why it does *not* conform to any of the principles described above.

History of graphology

The term graphology refers to two practices which are essentially different from one another: (1) the analysis of handwriting for the purpose of characterizing the personality of the writers, and (2) the analysis of handwriting for the purpose of identifying the authenticity of a written document or for the identification of the writer, a method employed mainly in criminal contexts. In this chapter, we will examine only the first type of graphology, namely that which pretends to analyze personality and traits of character. Most of the following historical information is taken from the comprehensive book edited by Beyerstein and Beyerstein, *The Write Stuff*.

Graphology was born in the seventeenth century. In 1622, the Italian philosopher and physician Camillo Baldi, published at the age of 70 the essay *Trattato Come Da Una Lettera Missiva Si Conoscano La Natura E Qualità Dello Scrittore* (*Treaty on How to Tell the Character and the Quality of a Person from His Handwriting*).[4] Baldi reprobated writers whose handwriting was flamboyant and artificial sustaining that it is impossible to learn anything about their "true" nature and inner life. He maintained that if the handwriting of a person is swift, equal, well-shaped and pleasure evoking, it was probably written by an ignorant, inconsequential person, for very rarely may we find wise people who write in an orderly manner. In contrast, he maintained that a handwriting which is inappropriate, poor, badly shaped, swift but readable suggests a mature person who is an experienced writer. But if the handwriting is not equal, and includes winding lines with a general uplifting inclination, it is obvious that the writer has a tendency to be controlling, and with such tendencies, it is also safe to assume that he has been stricken by cholera and is not in control of his instincts.

Baldi was a source of inspiration to a French Catholic clergy, which in 1830 initiated a study and interpretation of handwriting. The term graphology was coined by the French priest and archaeologist Jean-Hyppolite Michon, who, in 1872, founded in Paris the first society of graphology. Michon, perhaps because of his background in archaeology, adopted an analytical approach by which he attempted to systematically establish a link between certain signs in the handwriting (for example, the way the dot is shaped over the letter "i", and the way the line crosses over the letter "t", playful signs) and personality traits. This approach contrasted with the intuitive one practiced by the medieval Chinese philosophers such as Kuo Jo Hsu, as well as by other intellectuals in the eighteenth and nineteenth centuries, who, in their quest for a better understanding of the human psyche, believed that a close examination of one's handwriting leads to a better understanding of his/her personality. Despite the fact that Michon aspired to systematization (a requisite he believed would establish graphology as a science), his "fixed signs" were too numerous, arbitrary, and contradictory, and Michon made no attempt to resolve the contradictions by a more general theory of personality.

Michon's pupil, Crepieux-Jamin, broke away from his teacher's system and eventually adopted the *holistic approach*, maintaining that one example of writing must be examined and interpreted as a whole, where the signs and features are of unequal contribution. He believed that "the study of elements is to graphology as a study of the alphabet is to the reading of prose".

French researchers continued to dominate graphology until the end of the nineteenth century when the focus shifted to Germany. The German researcher Wilhelm Preyer attributed the physical characteristics of writing to psychological states and in 1895 defended the concept of handwriting being essentially "brain writing". This idea was based on the assumption that handwriting is a fundamentally stable characteristic of the individual notwithstanding its development over time; that its identifying core is preserved beyond the different means of writing – pen versus pencil, a page versus a board, writing not by the dominant hand and even foot writing. The German psychiatrist Georg Meyer outdid himself when he argued that writing, like all the other psychomotor functions, is an expression of emotion and suggested to add to graphology a new science, to be named "characterology". Meyer also attempted to create a vocabulary common to these two "scientific" fields, an ambition completed by Ludwig Klages, who put forth his theories in the five books he subsequently wrote. These books, as well as Klages himself, inspired an entire generation of German enthusiasts.

The Swiss writer, poet, and psychoanalyst Max Pulver extended Klages' theory to psychoanalysis. Pulver added to the usual measurements of the letter – height and width – also depth (i.e., the degree of pressure of the writing tool) which he attributed to the human libido. He also sought to evaluate the symbolic elements of handwriting and interpret them in a similar way to the symbolic interpretation of dreams. This ambition was fulfilled in his book *Symboliker der Handschrift* (*The Symbolism of Handwriting*), published in 1930. Pulver was interested in the unconscious and saw in the white blank paper a kind of potential world that may come into being through the individual's personality, be it in a swift but hesitant way, be it prolonged and subjected to a continuing examination of the past, be it enthusiastically and hurriedly, typical of some. He maintained that those whose handwriting is upward reaching are prone to sentimentality while the ones down reaching are of earthy natures. He believed that many of our drives are unconscious and that we are equally controlled – if not more – by our unconscious thoughts and emotions as well as by the conscious ones.

The list of graphology researchers and enthusiasts includes many more names across Europe and the US, and the rich past of graphology is well reflected in its present status. Numerous approaches compete for public attention. In the US alone, there are some 32 different graphology societies. Any title linked to graphology on Google will offer over 1.5 million entries. As opposed to the polygraph, which we examine in the next chapter, and which pretends to detect lies in a certain context, and insofar as personality goes, to detect the extent of honesty, the scope of personality traits that graphology claims to detect is almost infinite.

The use of graphology

The use of graphology is common mainly in the contexts of personnel screening and selection. In the vast, varied modern markets and all its organizations, businesses, institutions, and branches, on the one hand, and the countless candidates for each position on the other, the selection of suitable, qualified personnel is paramount. Due to the profusion and variety of functions, different functions tend to have specific requirements in order to achieve the maximum performance in each one of them. These are mostly listed in the description of the job requirements. Generally, these requirements refer both to cognitive aspects (intelligence, aptitude, and knowledge), as well as to character traits (honesty, integrity, leadership, entrepreneurship, teamwork, and so on).

Over the years, experts in the fields of organizational psychology and human resources have developed various mechanisms for assessing and measuring employees for the various existing capacities. For the measurement of the cognitive aspects, standard general aptitude tests have been developed – such as intelligence tests or tests that examine specific verbal or quantitative qualifications – and for the measurement of the personality aspects, objective personality tests (made up of multiple-choice questionnaires) and projection tests (such as sentence completion) have been developed. In addition, potential employers review the candidates' biographies, subject them to job interviews (sometimes more than just once), and seek letters of recommendation from previous places of employment and other experts.

In the twentieth century, graphology has also found its way into the toolbox of personnel selection. In 1965, insurance companies in the US had already examined the possibility of using handwriting analysis for personnel selection. In 1979, it was estimated that over 3,000 American insurance companies employed graphology to this end and that 85% of the companies in Europe used graphologists' recommendations as a routine. Nevertheless, the estimation of the extent to which graphology is used for personnel selection was based mainly on popular newspaper reports relying on the interviewees' opinions and not on systematic research that examined it empirically. The popularity of graphology stems from it being a simple means, less costly than others. There is no need to even convene the candidates except to acquire samples of their handwriting. In addition, graphology is not restricted to a single or a few personality traits and can assess the entire spectrum of personality. Some claim that the popularity of graphology for personnel selection increased in the US following the prohibition of the polygraph test to this end. If this assertion is true, then, as we will see later on, we have gone from bad to worse.

Ben-Shakhar and his colleagues (see the Bibliography) point out that in Israel, graphology is used for personnel selection more than any other professional personality test. Moreover, in Israel, graphology has been extended also for the selection of new members in *Kibbutzim* and *Moshavim*.[5] In an interview published by an Israeli newspaper with the most famous graphologist in Israel in 1990, she estimated that up until then, she had analyzed 250,000 samples of handwriting, among which were prestigious, well-known, important companies that we see no reason to name, for their names will mean nothing to our foreign readers. Today, Google yields for the entry "graphology" some 1,430,000 results, from which we may also learn of its popularity.

Is handwriting truly a mirror of our personality?

Apparently, handwriting is an appropriate candidate for analyzing the personality of its writers. Unlike the reading of palms, stars, and other objects, graphology relies on a concrete sample of an individual's behavior, which is a product of the self, and therefore could potentially express various personality traits. In addition, handwriting is unique, just as our personality is, and so the assumption that they might reflect each other is not altogether insensible. Handwriting is rich and diverse and includes many signs and characteristics, which is another reason why it is perceived as a tool that may characterize our personality, which is also very rich and complex. As mentioned before, handwriting is also a stable feature of the individual despite its development over time, just like our personality, which is relatively stable but also shifts and develops over time. However, if one views graphology as a scientific discipline, all these apparent similarities between handwriting and personality are not sufficient for validating graphology as a personality test. Only systematic research demonstrating robust relationships between handwriting features and personality traits could validate graphologists' claims.

From the literature we have read and from conversations we have entertained with graphologists, we have concluded that it is possible to classify graphology into two main categories: the "theoretical" approach and the "empirical" approach.

The "theoretical" approach

This approach links specific handwriting signs or a combination of signs, to personality traits. However, these links are based mainly on the use of the same adjectives to describe both the handwriting and the personality traits (e.g., handwriting with an upward tendency reflects optimism).

The clinical psychologist and graphologist James Crumbaugh reviews in Beyerstein and Beyerstein's book the approach known as "graphoanalysis" of which he is a follower, and which may be attributed to the theoretical approach. In this approach, two systems of traits are distinguished: the *primary* one, which may be typified by a single sign of handwriting, for example, the placement of the line on the letter "t", and the *evaluated* one, derived from two primary signs or more. Crumbaugh claims that a graphology analysis based on this system may discern many traits such as optimism, loyalty, logical thinking, impulsiveness, prejudice, diplomacy, selfishness, fears, and so on. But he does not believe that it may function as a physical or mental diagnostic tool. He is also doubtful of "graphotherapy", a movement that believes that the changing of the handwriting may impact the change of personality traits. To this effect, we would like to mention that when we wrote the book in Hebrew, we met with an Israeli graphologist who claimed that he had invented a computerized system for deciphering handwriting that enabled him to not only analyze personality traits but also diagnose physical illness. He claimed that he had diagnosed patients with heart disease before they were diagnosed by a physician.

According to Crumbaugh, handwriting is a system of graphic movements that contains information on the writer. This approach is based on the elementary assumption prevailing in clinical psychology and psychiatry that our personality is reflected in all our reactions to the environment, which may be summarized in two modes: the first one is verbal, in that we describe the way in which we interpret or perceive an ambiguous stimulus, such as a Rorschach ink blot[6]; the second one is motoric, in that our expressional movements are analyzed, for example, the drawing of a projective image or our handwriting. But Crumbaugh himself points out that the interpretation of the signs, which he believes is an attempt to link specific personality traits and signs or characteristics found in an ink blot or in handwriting, have never been validated, and that it is common to believe that the validation does not depend on the specific tool – such as the handwriting or ink blot – but on the testing clinician and the way he interprets the signs (just, as we will see, later on, is the case with the polygraph). Crumbaugh believes that the success of the interpretation depends on the experience and on the seniority of the clinician faced with the task of assembling – in a way that is categorically not analyzable – a comprehensive picture of the personality in question, drawn from the complex interaction between all the signs. By interaction he means that one sign (e.g., the size of the letter) will be assigned one interpretation when it appears with another sign (e.g., a handwriting with upward tendencies), and another interpretation when it appears without it (e.g., in a handwriting with downward inclinations). Crumbaugh claims that the holistic method, based on a global interpretation of all the signs that figure in the handwriting, is superior to the interpretation of the relationships between specific signs and personality traits.

In truth, what is termed by graphologists as "theory" is nothing more than the fact that it is possible to use similar or identical adjectives in order to describe both the writers' handwriting and their personality traits. In that, the essential theoretical assumption is that the possibility of characterizing handwriting and personality by the same adjectives is evidence of the correlations between them. Notwithstanding, some correlation *is* possible regarding general characteristics. For example, a sloppy handwriting could attest to a generally negligent, untidy person (albeit such handwriting may also result from syndromes such as attention deficit disorder and dyslexia); a very stylized handwriting may perhaps attest to some artistic talent; and an energetic, emphatic handwriting could belong to an energetic personality. Clearly, even these relatively simple hypotheses require empirical validation. Were these inferences valid, it would be relatively simple to explain them, for sloppy handwriting would be proof of a negligent person, artistic talent would be expressed in a stylized handwriting, and a high level of energy would, of course, be expressed also in motoric movements, among them, handwriting.

However, graphologists, as in Crumbaugh's case, claim to extract from handwriting much more than that. But what reason do we have to believe that complex personality traits such as honesty, leadership, empathy, selfishness, sadistic or masochistic tendencies, altruism, and social skills could have any manifestation in specific characterizations of the handwriting or, for the same matter, in any other physical motoric expression?

The "empirical" approach

This approach is not based on any "theory". Here, graphologists rely on a sample of handwriting belonging to people with a specific personality trait (e.g., people who have a reputation for being honest), and on an equivalent sample belonging to people with the opposite personality trait (i.e., dishonesty). Through the handwriting analysis of both samples, they attempt to detect the signs that differ between the two groups. These signs subsequently permit them to detect the personality trait in question (honesty, in this example). Some graphologists who support this approach believe that it is possible to apply it both to characterizing psychological traits, as well as to detecting physical conditions (i.e., diseases).

This approach has encountered serious difficulties that call its efficiency into question. To begin with, it is tremendously difficult to select large enough samples of people of whom we may be certain that they possess specific complex traits of character (morality, honesty, kindness, and so on). Second, even if we could surmount the first obstacle, detecting handwritten signs that distinguish between two groups of people that could be generalized beyond the specific sample requires cross-validation, a procedure that involves statistical skills and extensive sampling. What does this mean? Let us assume that we have detected through two handwriting samples some signs that distinguish between honest and dishonest people. For instance, the letter "n" ends in the honest ones' handwriting with an upward stroke and in the dishonest ones' in a downward stroke.

In order to make sure that this distinction is not arbitrary and that it does not reflect only these specific samples, we must choose two additional samples of honest and dishonest people's handwritings and repeat the same examination to see whether it yields the same results. The cross-validation is imperative, for the number of signs in one sample of handwriting is vast and it is possible to detect them in each letter of the alphabet, in the way that the writers attach the letters to words, the way the words are laid on the page, the size of the letters, their inclinations, the pressure of the pen and so on. Therefore, a comparison that is not guided by an a priori specific theory or assumption will result, with high probability, in an arbitrary set of distinguishing signs (out of the total number of possible signs) between the groups. Only a cross-validation procedure will tell us whether this set, selected on the basis of the initial samples, differentiates between honest and dishonest people in the new samples. From discussions we had with various graphologists, we learned that they were totally unaware of this problem. Moreover, graphologists do not think that they are obliged to validate or prove the inferences they make on the basis of handwriting analysis.

No doubt, many of us fall into the trap of *shifting the burden of proof*. We elaborate on what this means in our fifth chapter that deals with the topic of belief. For now, we will simply state that it is a prevalent human tendency to believe in anything under the sun unless there exists unequivocal evidence to refute it. However, scientific, critical thought places the burden of proof on whoever maintains the validity of the claim, in this case on the graphologists. In the scientific research literature, there are weak, if at all, links between motoric activity and handwriting movements. Even if any links had been found between the personality traits we have mentioned and characteristics of handwriting, it would still have been impossible to back them up with a sound theory. Furthermore, the fact that the handwriting is unique does not necessarily mean that it bears any relationship with any personality traits. Fingerprints are also unique for every individual, but no one would ever dream of suggesting that there exists a relationship between them and personality traits of their possessor.

Ultimately, the validity test must rely on both theoretical basis as well as empirical evidence. The theoretical basis of graphology, as we have pointed out, rests on the fact that it is possible to describe handwriting and personality traits with the same adjectives. This fact does not begin to constitute in any way a scientific theory. As far as the empirical evidence is concerned, we turn now to discuss controlled experiments which sought to examine the validity of the determination of personality traits, as well as the validity of predicting behavior, based on the analysis of handwriting.

The validity of graphology

In October 2010, the following story appeared on Ynet[7]:

> Ronen worked for over five years in Jonathan's company. His salary was raised and he was considered a professional popular employee. When the company's situation was compromised and Jonathan was forced to cut down on his staff, he found a new, "cheaper" candidate for the job, but not willing to pay Ronen severance, he did not quite know how to fire him. When he accidentally stumbled upon a report Ronen had written during a meeting, he decided to rip a page from Ronen's notebook. He handed it to a graphologist who worked with his company and asked him to examine the handwriting. The graphologist asserted, among other things, that Ronen "has a tendency for being disloyal". Jonathan could not believe his luck. He summoned Ronen for an immediate hearing, and fired him on the spot, pretending that "new evidence has been disclosed regarding his performance which is detrimental to the company". No more no less. The dumbfounded Ronen attempted to understand what

had happened, but Jonathan just told him that he'd best go home and not even imagine that he would be paid severance money.

Beyond the ethical problem that immediately arises in this story, in that, a graphological examination may not be performed without the consent of the person in question – a regulation that even appears in the list of regulations drawn by the *Israel Society of Graphology* – we are also faced with the need to establish the validity of this examination, whose results, as we have seen, may lead to the ruin of one's life. Considering the popularity of the use of graphology, especially in personnel selection, readers might be surprised to learn that the corpus of controlled scientific research done on graphology is rather meager. We would like to suggest a few explanations for this.

To begin with, because the practice of graphology is not institutionalized and is not anchored in any laws, it does not require any qualifications in basic science in general and in research methods in particular. As a result, most graphologists cannot conduct a study based on acceptable scientific standards. The various experimental psychologists, who might have examined the validity of graphology, for this is actually a personality test, have not expressed a special interest in it.

Second, there are many methodological difficulties in planning for such a study. We will list the most salient.

Comparison to reality

In order to be able to validate a graphologist's evaluation, we must compare it with reality, in that, we must test it against an independent uncontested criterion. For example, if a graphologist detects a personality trait such as honesty, we must compare this trait to the participants' honesty or dishonesty. In reality, it is next to impossible to verify complex personality traits, for these cannot be examined through direct systematic observations, and they also have multiple possible manifestations. People may be quite honest in one aspect of their lives and cheat in others. A scientist may be without reproach in what concerns his work and, at the same time, cheat on his spouse or in his income tax filing. Moreover, behavioral manifestations of complex personality traits may change from one situation to another. A person may be generally honest but may be tempted to transgressive behavior under severe financial hardship. In the distant past, personality researchers tended to test the manifestation of personality traits across a wide variety of situations. But following studies conducted by experimental psychologists – such as the Americans Walter Mischel, Richard Nisbett, and Lee Ross – we have come to understand that human behavior is much more complex than it was thought to be in the past, and that it is largely dependent on the individual's state of being at the time of the examination. The use of graphology, not unlike the use of many other psychological personality tests, is based on the attempt to infer, from the way people behave in a certain and rather narrow context – handwriting, for example – their personality, that is, their inclinations and behavior in totally different situations. Modern experimental psychology is fundamentally skeptical of this pretense. When a graphologist assesses that a person is dishonest based on his handwriting, the projection means that this person will exhibit dishonest behavior. But we will stress again that it is impossible to take this assertion seriously without taking into account the person's state of being at a given time.

The same criticism also applies to other psychological tests that claim to predict complex behavior based on personality questionnaires or projective tests, while ignoring situational factors. In the last decades, it has become common in personnel selection and screening to attribute significant weight to assessments based on simulated situations in which employees or future executives may find themselves. Ultimately, research studies conducted in organizational psychology on this topic show that simulating situations is better, as a rule, than the use of personality tests.

We might have attempted to overcome the difficulty we are discussing by comparing graphologists' evaluations with the results of personality tests. But given that the latter suffers from not too high a validity themselves, a lack of correlation would not necessarily attest to the feebleness of graphology. We could also imagine a comparison between graphological evaluations and subjective evaluations of people who have close knowledge of the candidates. But here also, the subjective evaluations are anything but reliable and therefore are not good contestants for generalizations.

Contamination of handwritten samples with biographical data

Generally, graphologists will analyze handwritten samples containing a lot of information about the candidates. Indeed, a standard requirement from the candidates is to supply a handwritten biography. Evidently, from this it is possible to extract ample information, relevant to the writer's tendencies and personality. Psychological research has shown that biographical data such as education, higher learning, and professional background may predict the extent of professional success. Therefore, it is impossible to tell if the graphologist's evaluation is based on the handwriting itself or is rather a reflection of the information present in the text. Moreover, texts which are not necessarily biographical and are written spontaneously may also inform us of the writers' verbal gifts or lack of them. Their vocabulary, eloquence (or lack of it), style, and general education may all supply valuable information to help predict the suitability of the candidates and their professional success. Graphologists maintain that they rely solely on the physical characteristics of the signs, but we are far from having any assurance that this is indeed the case and that they are not influenced by the textual content, whether they may be aware of it or not.

The proper way to examine the validity of the graphological evaluations would be to use standard textual samples (i.e., ask a few candidates to copy the same text). But most graphologists refuse to analyze such samples, claiming that they are of a poorer quality than that of spontaneous ones, without providing any explanation why the handwriting, considered by them to be time- and change-resistant, is for some reason not dependable when a text is being copied!

The difficulty in quantifying graphologists' evaluations

Graphologists tend to formulate handwriting analyses with rich personality descriptions written in a free manner. It is next to impossible to compare such descriptions with an independent criterion. This problem could be resolved through standardization of the graphologists' evaluations, that is, to shift to an evaluation system that would enable a quantitative scaling of the writers' handwriting in relation to a database of personality traits defined in advance – for example, setting a scale from 1 to 10 for defining honesty. But most graphologists refuse to work in this way. Another possibility suggested in the scientific literature would be to use "judges" who know the candidates well, such as close friends or relatives who would attempt to match the graphological evaluation to the candidates. But this suggestion is also not particularly feasible, for a systematic detection of sufficiently large random samples of writers, on the one hand, and groups of judges who have a close knowledge of them, on the other, is almost impossible.

However, albeit the methodological difficulties, the question of the relationship between the graphologists' evaluations that serve so many employers in personnel selection, and the extent of the chosen ones' success, needs to be addressed in order to examine whether its popular use is warranted. Of the existing research that has been published in scientific journals and was therefore rigorously reviewed, we have chosen to describe two experiments that were conducted in Israel in the occupational context by Ben-Shakhar and his colleagues.

In the first experiment, 80 handwritten samples were collected from the personal files of employees in two major banks in Israel. These files had been prepared by a reputable institute specializing in personnel selection and professional evaluation. The handwritten samples included short autobiographical descriptions. The files also included predictions prepared by the institute's psychologists based on cognitive and personality tests and other observations. Three graphologists employed by the institute volunteered to evaluate the handwritten samples and were explained the aims of the study. They were asked to evaluate the samples found in the files on an evaluation form according to three categories: (1) the level of aptitude and performance (e.g., the ability to learn from mistakes), (2) human interaction (e.g., readiness to give assistance to co-workers), and (3) loyalty and compliance with professional requirements (e.g., punctuality, respecting working hours). In addition, the form contained a summarizing item termed "general evaluation". Each category contained a few questions and each question offered a quantitative scale of 1 to 6. The validity criterion was the independent evaluation of the employees' direct superiors, which were measured according to the same categories. Because the handwritten samples included autobiographical information which could have indirectly helped the graphologists, the researchers used a clinical psychologist for control, who had no training whatsoever in graphology and who was also asked to evaluate the handwritten samples solely by their content. When they analyzed the results, the researchers examined the predictive validity of each graphologist against that of the clinical psychologist in relation to the validity criterion (the superiors' evaluations). As a rule, the predictive validity reflects the extent of correlation between the predictions and the validity criterion, and it is measured by a "correlation coefficient".[8]

Had there been any truth in the argument that the graphological evaluations contain information which can predict occupational success, one would expect to obtain a higher correlation between the graphologists' evaluations and those of the direct superiors, than between the psychologist's evaluations and the direct superiors. But the results obtained in this study pointed to the exact opposite. While all correlation coefficients were only slightly higher than 0, the clinical psychologist was more successful in her predictions than any of the graphologists, that is, her predictive validity was higher than that of all the graphologists. The graphologists' predictive validity was lower not only than that of the clinical psychologist but also than that of the evaluations made by the institute's psychologists in the employees' files. Furthermore, the addition of the graphologists' evaluation to those provided by the evaluation institute did not in the least increase the predictive validity.

To obtain an additional control, the experimenters asked two students without any background in graphology to analyze the content in the handwritten samples and grade them according to biographic variables: education, military rank, seniority in Israel, family status, and personal preferences. In addition, they were asked to grade the quality of the text, its lingual mistakes, esthetics, and finally, their general impression. It was found that the validity of these variables put together was much higher than the predictive validity of each of the three graphologists. In particular, the quality of the text variable alone scored a much higher predictive validity than any of the three graphologists.

The second experiment conducted by Ben-Shakhar and his colleagues was unique, in that graphologists were exceptionally willing to use standard handwritten samples devoid of any biographical information. Five extremely experienced graphologists participated in this experiment; all of them worked with handwritten material in Hebrew, all of them enjoyed a steady stream of clients, and all of them considered graphology their main occupation, if not the only one. At least three of them had achieved public acclaim through books they had published on graphology, interviews in the media, and radio shows in which they manifested their talents. More than 12 other graphologists were invited to participate in the experiment but they refused. It was agreed with the graphologists that the handwritten samples would include the following items: (1) copying a whole page from a book by Ephraim Kishon (a famous Israeli satirist); (2) copying the saying, "If I'm not for myself – who is for me and if not now, when"? three consecutive times; (3) writing down from their memory a very well-known Israeli nursery rhyme, named "Little Jonathan"; (4) copying four arithmetic exercises and their solutions; (5) writing along a few lines the letters M and O, alternately; (6) writing numbers 1–10 three times; and (7) signing a made-up name (Yigal Ben-Israel) in the closest possible way to the participants' own signature. The participants were asked to write the tasks in pencil on a lineless page handed out by the researchers.

The participants included 40 men whose initial written language was Hebrew. They represented eight different professional fields: mathematics, clinical psychology, philosophy, painting, chemical engineering administration, architecture, surgical medicine, and law. All of them were prominent in their fields, had practiced it for their entire professional lives (at least for 10 years), and expressed great satisfaction with their professional choices. Their colleagues described them as "successful". From all this, we may deduce that they were indeed suitable to their professions.

The graphologists were handed the list of the professions and were told that each writer belongs to one profession only. Their task was to match the handwritten samples to the professions. They were not limited by any number of professions that could be assigned to each writer (as one person may be apt for a few professions). In addition, they were allowed to skip professions that seemed to them undetectable from handwriting, and also to avoid evaluating samples that seemed to them non-interpretable. A "correct" classification was when a graphologist assigned to a participant his correct profession. The statistical analysis compared the percentage of correct conjectures of each graphologist with the percentage of correct conjectures expected in a random prediction model (for example, by lottery), considering the total number of classifications provided by the same graphologist for each handwritten sample. The results of the statistical analysis showed that not even one of the five graphologists' predictions was significantly higher than what would have been obtained by a random model, that is to say, through a lottery or a coin flip.

One might argue that the failure of the three graphologists in the first experiment and the failure of the five in the second one to correctly predict professional suitability does not necessarily attest to the failure of graphology as a discipline. Indeed, as we emphasize time and time again, one of the principles of reliable observations is the need to obtain identical results in repeated experiments. It is therefore unsatisfactory to settle for one or two experiments before we pronounce the verdict of graphology.

In many scientific fields, it is common to conduct once in every few years a meta-analytical study, that is, a statistical survey and analysis of the results obtained in *all* the experiments conducted on a particular question to date. For example, in the medical field, suppose we wish to examine the efficiency of a drug for temperature control. In a single experiment, the question is examined by a comparison of a group that has been given the drug with a group that has been given a placebo. The measure will, of course, be by how much the temperature of those who have been administered the drug decreased in comparison with the control (the placebo) group. The result of this comparison is known as "the effect size". In a meta-analytical study, the effect sizes that have been obtained in a large number of experiments are analyzed statistically, the average effect size is calculated, and an attempt is made to explain the differences obtained in the effect sizes in the different experiments.

In the studies conducted in the field of personnel selection, the question usually examined is the prediction quality of the various classification tools (intelligence tests, personality tests, and graphology). In such studies, the effect size measure is the correlation coefficient between the predictor (the graphologist's evaluation, for example) and the criterion (the superiors' evaluations). As we have pointed out, in the field of graphology, the number of existing experiments is relatively small so that it is hard to conduct a sound meta-analytical study.

The only meta-analytical study of graphology known in the professional literature was conducted in Israel in 1989. The researchers surveyed all the studies that examined the prediction validity of graphology in personnel selection published up until then, as well as relevant studies that had not been published, such as MA theses from various universities. Of all the studies, 17 were found conforming to all the criteria for meta-analysis. These included 63 graphologists and 51 "non-graphologists" (that constituted the control) who evaluated a total of 1,223 handwritten samples. Of the 17 studies, only two used standard texts devoid of biographical content. The results of the meta-analysis were very similar to the ones reported by Ben-Shakhar and his colleagues, described above. In that, the predictive validity of the graphologists who worked with the samples that included content was slightly higher than 0, but it was not higher than that of the non-graphologists. In the two cases where the graphologists analyzed standard texts, the predictive validity was 0.

To the above meta-analysis, the researcher Geoffrey Dean contributed three more studies which have not altered the picture in the least bit. Dean also compared the validity of the graphological evaluations with 15 other methods and variables used in the prediction of occupational success such as cognitive tests, evaluation centers, interviews, and age. The obtained results showed that graphology was the worst predictor in comparison with all the other methods and variables, except the age variable. Dean himself conducted an additional meta-analysis in which he examined the predictive validity of graphological evaluations against the criterion of personality tests or personality evaluations – both self-evaluations and evaluations by others. He summarized his findings as follows: (1) the predictive validity is too low to be useful, (2) the predictive validity of the graphologists is not higher than that of non-graphologists, and (3) the predictive validity decreases when standard texts are used.

Therefore, it would not be an exaggeration to assert that the amusing quotations we cited at the beginning of this chapter constitute a shining demonstration of the graphologists' manner of working: the conclusions supposedly drawn from the analyses of the handwritten samples reflect nothing more than information previously obtained about the writers or simply the contents of the texts. It is no accident that they insist on examining "authentic" handwritten samples that include significant information pertaining to the writers.

However, the results obtained in the above-described studies demonstrating that the graphologists' claims to be able to detect personality traits and predict occupational success are completely unfounded have not discouraged either the graphologists or their clients. We elaborate on the question of belief on the part of the suppliers, as well as on the part of the clients in the last chapter of our book. For now, will mention Dale Beyerstein's claim that the burden of proof regarding the validity of any method rests on those claiming its validity and certainly not on the skeptics. Beyerstein asserts that the graphology defenders hasten to contend that "all" that the skeptics manage to prove in experiments such as those we have reviewed is that a particular hypothesis has been refuted, that a particular group of graphologists has not managed to demonstrate its skills in a particular experiment, and that from this evidence alone, we cannot generalize that graphology is worthless. He compares this to his admission that "all" that he has been able to prove about the existence of Santa Claus is that he has never come down *his* chimney, but given that none of his friends have reported a visit, and that he has reasons to suspect reports that Santa Claus has visited other people, and that there are theoretical reasons for finding this existence claim implausible, his skepticism regarding Santa Claus is more than just a peculiar prejudice! So, the onus of proof is on the believer of Santa Claus and not on the skeptics.

Such is the case with graphology. In the absence of positive results from controlled experiments conducted by the believers or graphology practitioners, the negative results presented by the researchers/skeptics constitute very strong evidence. For as long as we do not have an objective, standardized system for graphological evaluation, discussing graphology independently of its practitioners is futile.

Finally, we would like to stress that a strong belief in something is not necessarily connected to any scientific empirical evidence of its validity. Belief is nice and well so long as it does not do any harm each one of us after their own heart inclinations. But when the belief in something leads us as individuals or as a society to commit errors which may have devastating repercussions, we had better know/learn what lies – or rather does not lie – behind such a belief.

Notes

1 Mordechai Vanunu was an Israeli nuclear technician who revealed information regarding Israel's nuclear weapons program to the British press in the 1980s. He was tried for high treason and spent 18 years in the Israeli prison.
2 These principles rely mostly on the ones offered by Stanovich in his book and by Lilienfeld and his colleagues in theirs (see the references).
3 Singh and Ernst provide in their book *Trick or Treatment* a thorough definition of a controlled medical experiment, including the placebo effect, as well as its history.
4 It has not been published in English.
5 Two forms of rural communal settlements in Israel.
6 The Rorschach is a projective psychological test. The participants receive various forms of ink blots known as "The Rorschach Test" (after the Swiss psychiatrist Herman Rorschach who invented the test in 1921) and are required to list the thoughts that they associate with the ink blots.
7 Israeli news website owned by *Yedioth Group*, which is the largest media company in Israel.

8 The *correlation coefficient* is a statistical measure that describes the strength of the linear relationship between two variables. Its values range between (–1) and (+1).

The correlation is +1 when there is a full positive correlation between the two variables (i.e., increase of one variable is accompanied by a parallel increase of the other); the correlation is –1 when there is a full negative correlation between the two variables (i.e., increase in one variable is accompanied by a parallel decrease in the other); correlation 0 reflects a total lack of correlation between the two variables.

Bibliography

Bar-Hillel, M., & Ben-Shakhar, G. (1986). The a priori case against graphology: Methodological and conceptual issues. In: B. Nevo (Ed.), *Scientific Aspects of Graphology*. Springfield, IL: Charles C. Thomas, 263–279.

Ben-Shakhar, G., Bar-Hillel, M., Bilu, Y., Ben-Abba, E., & Flug, A. (1986). Can graphology predict occupational success? Two empirical studies and some methodological ruminations. *Journal of Applied Psychology, 71,* 645–653.

Beyerstein, B.L., & Beyerstein, D.F. (Eds.) (1992) *The Write Stuff: Evaluation of Graphology—The Study of Handwriting Analysis.* Amherst, NY: Prometheus.

Crepieux-Jamin, J. (1926). *The Psychology of the Movements of Handwriting* (trans., and arranged by L.K. Given-Wilson). London, UK: Routledge.

Crumbaugh, J.C. (1992). Graphoanalytic cues. In: B.L. Beyerstein & D.F. Beyerstein (Eds.), *The Write Stuff: Evaluation of Graphology—The Study of Handwriting Analysis.* Amherst, NY: Prometheus.

Crumbaugh, J.C., & Stockholm, E. (1977). Validation of graphoanalysis by "global" or "holistic" method. *Perceptual and Motor Skills, 44,* 403–410.

Dean, G.A. (1992). The bottom line: Effect size. In: B.L. Beyerstein & D.F. Beyerstein (Eds.), *The Write Stuff: Evaluation of Graphology—The Study of Handwriting Analysis.* Amherst, NY: Prometheus.

Lilienfeld, S.O., Lynn, S.J., & Lohr, J.M. (2003). *Science and Pseudoscience in Clinical Psychology.* New York: Guilford Press.

Lilienfeld, S.O., Lynn, S.J., Ruscio, J., & Beyerstein, B.L. (2010). *50 Great Myths of Popular Psychology: Shattering Widespread Misconceptions about Human Behavior.* Chichester, West Sussex, UK: Wiley-Blackwell.

Mischel, W. (1976). *Introduction to Personality*. New York: Holt, Rinehart and Winston.

Neter & Ben-Shakhar (1989). The predictive validity of graphological inferences: A meta-analytic approach. *Personality and Individual Differences, 10*, 737–745.

Nisbett, R. E., & Ross, L. (1980). *Human Inference: Strategies and Shortcomings of Social Judgment*. Englewood Cliffs, NJ: Prentice Hall.

Pulver, M. (1931). *Symbolik der Handschrift*. Zurich, Switzerland: Orell Fussli.

Singh, S., & Ernst, E. (2009). *Trick or Treatment?: Alternative Medicine on Trial*. New York: W.W. Norton & Company Ltd.

Stanovich, K.E. (2001). *How to Think Straight About Psychology* (6th ed.). Boston, MA: Allyn and Bacon.

4

Pinocchio's nose
The truth behind the lie detector

Oops, an innocent man has been condemned to life imprisonment

We shall begin this chapter with a story provided by the American psychologist David T. Lykken in his excellent book, *A Tremor in the Blood: Uses and abuses of the Lie Detector*.[1]

March 29, 1978. It is 4 o'clock in the morning. Floyd Fay, known to all as "Buzz", a Conrail employee, is awaken in his trailer home in Pittsburgh, Ohio, by a loud banging on his door. When he opens the door, he is faced with several policemen, guns drawn, and is arrested immediately for aggravated murder. An acquaintance of Buzz, Fred Ery, manager of "Andy's Carry-Out", had been murdered the previous night by a man wearing a ski mask and carrying a sawed-off shotgun. To the question who he thought might have been his assailant, Ery replied, sedated for pain and having lost much blood, "It looked like Buzz but it couldn't have been". Several hours later, while dying, he changed his version to "Buzz did it". The house search procured neither a shotgun nor a ski mask. Furthermore, an eye-witness claimed that the ski jacket found in Fay's trailer was not the same one the shooter was wearing. Fay's sole prior offense was a ticket for drunk driving.

But after a week of unproductive investigation, the police offered to drop the charges against Fay, provided he admitted to guilt if found so by a polygraph examination. Ill-advised by his defenders, Fay agreed and was found guilty by the polygraph test (as we shall see, this kind of test is not usually admissible in criminal courts). The district attorney showed special magnanimity and brought in a second polygraphist to test Fay. But the second polygraphist also asserted that Fay was deceptive. During the trial, no evidence was presented that might have refuted the polygraph test results. Fay was found guilty of aggravated murder, and the only solace his attorney could provide was the fact that the death penalty that had been the sentence for this kind of crime, had been proclaimed unconstitutional by the Ohio Supreme Court shortly beforehand. Fay was sentenced for life. From his prison cell, he wrote to Lykken, who is an uncompromising critic of the polygraph method employed in the Fay case (on which we elaborate later on), and asked him for reprints of his scholarly articles. Meanwhile, Fay also employed the services of a young ambitious public defender. Lykken offered to give expert testimony if the attorney would manage to obtain a new trial. But the attorney outdid himself: he investigated the details of the case himself, and after 2 years, he managed to obtain a confession from the driver of the getaway car, who named the real shooter. Fay was exonerated and walked out of prison a free man.

Although we may conclude that the above story has a fair end – for 2 years in prison beat a life sentence – a completely innocent man was sent to prison as a result of two unfortunate polygraph tests. This is an outrageous occurrence, to say the least. But how is it possible that a machine such as the polygraph (also known as lie detector) – which is allegedly based on scientific principles – yields two consecutive erroneous results? In this chapter, we examine this question in depth, as well as demonstrate how far-reaching the consequences of false polygraph tests may be.

Lying, honesty, and the desire to tell them apart

> One man cheats the other,
> They will not speak truth;
> They have trained their tongues to speak
> Falsely;
>
> Jeremiah, 9:4

> A truthful witness saves lives;
> He who testifies lies spreads deceit.
>
> Proverbs, 14:25

As Lykken points out in his book, the propensity to lie is inherent in the human nature and stems from an evolutionary drive. People lie from the minute they learn how to express themselves, and lying transcends social class, cultures, age, and gender. We show gratitude for a present we do not need; flatter our hosts for a sumptuous dinner that almost got stuck in our throats; children often lie to their parents – on grades, on their whereabouts, and what not; parents will often lie to their children for various reasons – to threaten them, to scare them, to save unnecessary expenses, or alternatively to protect them, to flatter them, to build up their self-confidence, and so on.[2]

Notwithstanding, lying is perceived as subversive and harmful, and so normative human behavior excludes it. This is one of the more fascinating sociocultural discrepancies our society lives with, and it has always preoccupied and continues to preoccupy innumerable researchers in various fields, such as philosophy, religious studies, sociology, psychology, and law. How can we have a social norm that contradicts our natural inclinations? Why do we lie when we know that lying is bad, and not only when we are forced to in order to protect someone's feelings? Moreover, why don't we always mind when we are being lied to? It seems that very often we bury our heads in the sand in order to protect our own feelings. Not always will uncovering the truth work in our favor. Very often, the lies are better – why should we bother to examine the truth behind a wonderful compliment we have received that has made our day?

The Israeli psychologist Eitan Elaad remarks that studies show that we do indeed lie a lot and we do so once a day on average, mostly telling "white lies". Furthermore, liars do not feel remorse for having told such lies and maintain that they would repeat them under similar circumstances. From this, we may conclude that some lies are not only innocuous but quite the contrary, they are vital to maintaining sound social order as well as interpersonal relationships. However, this is not the case when "serious" lies are concerned which are detrimental to society.

The ease with which human beings lie on the one hand, and the harm that may be inflicted on society as a result of critical lies on the other, are probably what gave birth to the need to distinguish between truth speakers and liars, including the need – perhaps even the necessity – to anchor this distinction in lawful systems that include penalty.

From time immemorial, people in all cultures and societies have aspired to develop means of distinction between liars and truth-tellers while firmly believing that this ambition may indeed materialize. Who has not heard of Carlo Collodi's famous children's story of Pinocchio, an animated wooden marionette, whose nose grows bigger every time he lies? What could demonstrate this ambition better? The Hindus used to make suspected liars chew rice and then spit it out on a ficus leaf, which was considered holy. If the rice stuck on it, the suspect was proclaimed truthful; but how bitter was the fate of those whose rice did not land successfully on the ficus leaf because it stuck on their tongue or their palate. During the Spanish Inquisition, a similar method was applied to examine the clergy's faithfulness. The rice was replaced with bread and cheese, which was placed on the altar in front of the suspected priest. If the food stuck in his throat it was proof of his guilt. According to Eitan Elaad, some Bedouin tribes to this day practice a rite whereby suspects are required to draw their tongue across a white-hot iron spoon. If the tongue is scorched the suspect is considered untruthful. In Chapter 5 of the *Book of Numbers*, we may find the sacral water test. If someone suspects that his wife is being adulterous, he must bring her to the priest, who will pour sacral water into an earthen vessel, mix it with earth taken from the tabernacle and have her drink it. If her belly distends and her thigh sags, it means that she has had carnal relations with another.

All of the above examples are methods that preceded the modern polygraph, for they all rely on the same principle: fear and nervousness activate the autonomic nervous system, responsible for involuntary activity, including mouth drying. But who will not fear and tremble before a test such as those we have mentioned? Nevertheless, the assumption implicit in all these methods is that because the suspects believe wholeheartedly in these methods' ability to distinguish between liars and truth-tellers, the truth-tellers will be confident that their righteousness will prevail, and therefore, they will have nothing to fear. As we will read in this chapter, this is also one of the assumptions that guides the modern popular polygraph test.

Contrary to the common belief that it is simple to tell a liar by his facial expressions or body language, studies have shown that in most cases, the accuracy of such diagnoses is not much higher than chance. Similar findings were obtained among professionals whose work requires such identifications (police officers, judges, psychiatrists, and polygraphists). This is precisely what begot the need to invent a smart machine to which to assign this task.

The idea of a lie-detection machine based on measuring physiological responses sparked the human imagination for a long time precisely because these responses are perceived as non-voluntary. The assumption is that someone who manages to hide the fact that he is lying in a regular human interaction will be betrayed by his involuntary physiological responses. But as we shall see, this assumption is not accurate, for it is possible to control most of these responses, at least partially. Another factor motivating modern society to design such a machine stems from the desire to avoid violent investigative methods involving physical, mental, and psychological torture which are not only inhuman but also very often lead to false admissions. Unfortunately, these methods have not perished from our world, and in any case, the use of the polygraph, as we will see, does not impede false admissions.

The modern polygraph then is a tool that measures simultaneously a number of physiological responses to a series of questions presented to the suspect. Today, the polygraph is used not only in the criminal context but also for security screening and personnel classification. Hence, we may identify two main categories in the use of the polygraph: in the first, the test refers to a specific incident or event and its purpose is to check whether the suspect was involved in it. A typical example of this use is indeed the criminal context, i.e., checking whether the suspect is involved in a theft. We may term this *the event-related use*. In the second category, the purpose of the test is to examine the examinees' credibility in general, rather than their involvement in a specific event. A typical example of this use is personnel classification for highly classified positions or other positions requiring a high level of integrity. We may term this *the non-event-related use*.

The truth will out: a brief history of the polygraph

At the end of the nineteenth century, the Italian criminologist and physician Cesare Lombroso developed a device for examining changes in the human blood pressure and pulse, similar to one of the measures used in the modern polygraph. However, the modern polygraph was born in the US, where it is still widespread, or as Lykken says, not any less American than apple pie.

In 1908, Hugo Münsterberg, a psychology professor at Harvard University, published a book surveying various methods of lie detecting based on experimental psychology. His student, William Moulton Marston, developed during the 1920s and 1930s a device also based on measuring changes in blood pressure. Marston truly believed that his device would put an end to the continual failed attempts to develop a tool that would distinguish between lying and truth-telling. He was also among the first to recognize the commercial potential of such a machine. Lykken points out that he was also the one who either coined the term "lie detector" or borrowed it from one of the journalists to whom he described the wonders of this machine.

Marston is also known for his invention of the character Wonder Woman – who started her career in comics and went on to feature in American films and television series – whose magic golden lasso served her in her efforts for a better and juster society. Those caught in Wonder Woman's lasso lost their ability to lie, and she used her lasso to extract guilt admissions and impose order. Similar to the polygraph, which was the golden lasso's source of inspiration, the lasso's purpose was to establish the truth and, consequently, bring about justice and freedom. This invention is most probably the initiative of Marston's wife, Elizabeth, who was a feminist and shared his work. Marston himself believed that his experiments showed women to be more reliable and truthful than men and capable of producing more effective and accurate work.

The forensic American psychiatrist John A. Larson developed in the 1930s the first polygraph that measured simultaneous changes in blood pressure and breathing. His polygraph served in criminal investigations in the state of California, but Lykken stresses the fact that Larson himself remained skeptical regarding its reliability.

At the early stages, the polygraph engineers understood that in order for the machine to detect lying, measuring physiological responses alone would not suffice and that it would be necessary to develop a method to formulate questions as well as to interpret the responses to draw conclusions. Particularly, it was not sufficient to examine the suspect's physiological responses to a specific question but also to compare his various responses to different types of questions. This realization was induced by two main factors: first, all the responses measured by the polygraph are responses that reflect arousal or excitement but not their **specific cause**, which remains obscure. For example, a strong response may be elicited as a result of surprise or cognitive effort. Hence, the conclusion that one lies will necessarily be indirect. Second, there are significant interpersonal differences in the physiological responses and in their magnitude so that a certain physiological response may be relatively strong in one person and weaker in another. Hence, all the investigative questions that were designed in the course of time are based on a comparison between the suspects' responses to two types of questions that will be termed **relevant questions** and **control questions**.

The relevant/irrelevant questions test

The polygraph interrogation methods developed by Marston, Larson, and others relied on comparing the physiological responses to relevant questions, i.e., direct questions relating to the felony (for example, "Did you help rob Mr. Brown's jewelry shop"?) with totally neutral questions (for example, "Are you wearing a shirt"?). This method was termed the Relevant/Irrelevant Test, or shortly, the R/I Test. An examinee who responded more strongly to the relevant questions than the irrelevant ones was classified as liar or guilty.

This method is evidently absurd, for even an innocent suspect who is interrogated at the police station while tied to a polygraph machine will be frightened and therefore respond more strongly to the relevant questions than to a neutral, innocent question such as "Are you wearing a shirt"? or "Is your name Johns"? Notwithstanding, until the 1950s, this was the standard interrogation polygraph test in the US.

How did its practitioners justify it? They relied on at least one of the following two assumptions: (1) the sheer telling of a lie is typified by unique physiological responses, and (2) the examinees have complete confidence in the machine's reliability. The first assumption reflects the belief that the polygraph acts as Pinocchio's nose, that is, whenever someone lies in response to a relevant question, it will immediately show in his physiological responses (of course, his response to the irrelevant question will be truthful). Again, this assumption has absolutely no empirical evidence; on the contrary, much evidence points to the fact that all the responses measured by the polygraph reflect various psychological factors that have nothing to do with lying (e.g., surprise, mental effort).

The second assumption reflects the belief that the innocent suspect, who firmly believes in the polygraph, is confident that his innocence (the truth) will out, and therefore is not in the least intimidated by the relevant questions, so that his responses to both the relevant and irrelevant questions will be similar. This assumption is also unfounded, for people may certainly doubt the police's ability – the polygraph included – to solve crimes, as we have learned of many cases in which people have been falsely accused. Furthermore, even those who believe in the polygraph are likely to respond more strongly to the relevant questions which are, by nature, more inflammatory than the irrelevant ones.

Since the 1950s, the use of the R/I Test in criminal investigations was gradually stopped; however, it is still practiced in personnel security screening and classification, as we shall see.

The comparison question test (CQT)

At the end of the 1940s, the American lawyer John E. Reid developed a method that replaced the R/I Test. Reid founded a school (The Reid School of Detection of Deception) which trained many polygraphists in the United Stated and elsewhere. Their qualification was a master's degree after a course of instruction that lasted only 6 months). Together with Fred Inbau, a law professor at the Northwestern University, Reid published the book *Truth and Deception: The Polygraph "Lie Detector" Technique*, which for many years served as the polygraphists' bible. Reid's method was termed the Control Question Test, or in short the CQT. In due course, the name was altered to the Comparison Question Test. This became the polygraph's standard interrogation test in criminal investigations.

In this test, in addition to the relevant and irrelevant questions described above, the suspect is also asked control (or comparison) questions. These questions relate to general information regarding the suspect's past life and are believed to arouse emotional responses. As a rule, the comparison questions are of the same nature as the relevant ones, so that in a case of theft, for example, if the relevant question is "Have you stolen the jewelry"?, the comparison question would be something similar to "Have you stolen anything in the past 5 years"? Thus, the determination of deception is based on comparing the suspect's physiological responses to the relevant questions with his physiological responses to the comparison questions. The irrelevant questions do not play any part in the weighting of the ultimate decision (truth/deception) but are presented to the suspect at the beginning of the investigation in order to absorb the **orienting response**, which is the response we have to any new stimulus regardless of its content. If the suspect responds more strongly to the relevant questions (i.e., "Have you stolen the jewelry"?) than to the comparison questions (i.e., "Have you stolen anything in the past 5 years"?) the test will conclude that he is deceptive. The opposite pattern of responses will motivate the polygraphist to conclude that the suspect is telling the truth.

The logic behind this **decision rule** relies on the following assumptions: when suspects respond negatively to the comparison question, they are either lying or at least not sure of their answer. Therefore, the innocent suspect will dread the comparison question more than the relevant one (to which he replied truthfully) and will physically respond accordingly. In contrast, the guilty suspect, even if he dreads both questions, will be more affected by the relevant question pertaining to the crime he has committed. Before we attack the problems inherent in these assumptions, we shall now describe the process of a typical polygraph Comparison Question Test, which from now onward will be referred to as the CQT.

In the criminal context, the CQT is conducted in several stages: first, the polygraph investigator studies the details of the event in question by reading all pertinent reports and by conversing with the police officers who commissioned the test. As a rule, he is informed of any piece of information that seems relevant, including information from the suspect's history. In the second stage, the investigator conducts a pretest interview in which the suspect is given the opportunity to speak freely about the event and provide his own version. The investigator explains to the suspect the process of the test and makes sure that the suspect is in agreement with it, for his consent is mandatory. The primary objective of this pretest interview is to enable the investigator to formulate – through conversing with the suspect – the questions that will be asked during the test itself. Among other things, the investigator aims to formulate the comparison questions in a way that will leave the suspect prone to answering them negatively, which is a necessity in the CQT. Let us demonstrate this with the comparison question, "Have you stolen anything from your employer in the past 5 years"? If during the pretest interview the suspect admits to having stolen something, then the investigator will change the comparison question to "Have you stolen anything from your employer in the past 5 years, outside the object to which you have admitted"?

Another objective – albeit concealed – of the pretest interview is to blur the distinction between the relevant questions relating directly to the suspect's involvement in the crime and the comparison questions relating to his past in general. This is because the CQT relies, among other things, on the premise that the suspect is not aware of the polygraph investigator's decision rule, namely that a relatively strong response to the relevant questions will incriminate him, while a relatively strong response to the comparison questions will exonerate him (as we shall see, this assumption is not plausible). The belief is that once a suspect is aware of the decision rule, he will have no reason to fear the comparison questions which act in his favor; if truthful or innocent suspects are aware of the decision rule, they too are likely to fear only the relevant questions and will therefore respond more strongly to them and be consequently ruled as deceptive (we shall demonstrate this point later on in this chapter).

The third stage of the CQT is the test itself, during which the suspect is connected to the machine. As a rule, three physiological measures are monitored: changes in breathing, which are measured by pneumatic tubes positioned around the thoracic area and around the abdomen; changes in skin conductance measured by electrodes connected to two of the suspect's fingers; and changes in relative blood pressure measured by a blood pressure cuff attached to the upper arm of the suspect. At this stage, the investigator does his best to convince the suspect of the polygraph's precision. To this end, he gives the suspect a card test in which the suspect is required to choose a numbered card from a card stack and conceal it from the investigator. The investigator then asks the suspect a few times, "Have you picked card X"? and names a different number each time until he identifies the chosen card allegedly by the suspect's physiological responses to the various cards. In truth, to make sure that the identification is correct, the investigators have means to know the identity of the card beforehand, while the suspect, of course, is unaware of it. The card test may be conducted before the test itself or during the test, in the breaks between the various sets of questions.

The polygraph CQT itself comprises approximately ten questions: three to four relevant questions, three to four comparison questions, and two to three irrelevant questions. The questions are presented consecutively, allowing approximately 20 seconds in between. The entire set of questions is presented to the suspect at least three times.

In the fourth stage, the examiner analyzes the test results. In both the R/I Test and the CQT described above, the examiner's conclusion that the suspect is truthful or deceptive is based on the **examiner's interpretation**.

The CQT's results have been often evaluated by the **global evaluation method**, in which the examiner checks all the polygraph charts weighting the differences in the responses to the relevant questions against those to the comparison questions and draws his conclusion accordingly. A more elaborate and standardized chart scoring method was introduced by Cleve Backster, who was among Reid's first students. Backster became known when he experimented with plants that he attached to the polygraph.

He believed that the plants' reactions were affected by the various substances in the lab in which they were placed, including Backster's own presence. His method was termed the **zone of comparison**. It is based on a systematic comparison between responses to pairs of relevant and comparison questions presented to the suspect in contiguity. These comparisons are examined separately for each polygraph channel (physiological measure). The scores awarded to each pair range between −3 and +3. The positive scores are awarded when the response to the comparison question is estimated as stronger than the one to the relevant question, and the negative scores are awarded when the response to the relevant question is estimated as stronger than the one to the comparison question. The score 0 is awarded when the examiner estimates that there is no difference between the two responses. The numerical values indicate the examiner's evaluation regarding the magnitude of the difference between the two categories of responses (score 1 represents a small difference, score 2 represents a medium difference, and score 3 represents a strong difference).

At the end of this process, the examiner sums up all the numerical values received in the individual comparisons. For example, when the series of questions includes three pairs of relevant and comparison questions, and it is repeated four times while the three physiological responses are measured, there will be 36 comparisons (3 pairs of questions times 4 repetitions, times 3 physiological measures) and the sum score will range between −108 and +108. In this method, the decision rule is obtained as follows: When the sum score is higher than +5, the suspect is classified as truthful (no deception indicated); when the sum score is lower than −5, the suspect is classified as deceptive; when the sum score ranges between −5 and +5, the test results are classified as inconclusive.

As we have already pointed out, in the US, the CQT as described above has become the standard polygraph test in criminal investigations. But it has been extended to other countries as well, and besides the US, it is very popular in Canada and Israel. In European countries, the use of the polygraph is uncommon, even though in the past decade there has been increased use in some countries, especially in Finland and Belgium.

In Israel, as well as in other countries, the CQT is not admissible as evidence in criminal courts; nevertheless, police investigators use it extensively, particularly when the police lacks substantial evidence for an indictment. When polygraph examiners conclude that the suspect is truthful, the police usually turns to other lines of investigation. However, when the polygraph examiner is under the impression that the suspect is lying, the latter is pressured to admit to his culpability. So even if the polygraph test results are not admissible in criminal court as evidence, the admittance of guilt as a result of a polygraph test *is* admissible. However, admissions obtained as a result of pressure may be false. Indeed, there is extensive documentation, particularly in the US, of cases in which innocent people have admitted to a crime in the course of a police investigation. Apparently, this phenomenon contradicts any basic logic, for, why would a suspect admit to a crime he has not committed? The American psychologist Saul M. Kassin and his colleagues have studied the topic and classified it into three categories. First, false admissions are given willingly, particularly by people who seek fame in the context of widely covered affairs. One example they give is the kidnapping of the aviation pioneer Charles Lindbergh's son in the US in 1932, for which 200 people claimed responsibility. Second, false admissions obtained as a result of exercising physical and psychological pressure in police investigations – in these instances, people admit to culpability in order to put an end to the pressure (for example, to be able to sleep after extended sleep deprivation, or to be able to eat after extended food deprivation). In such situations, people assign an advantage to the immediate relief at the expense of a heavy price they might pay in the long run, because – among other things – they are confident that the justice system will ultimately prove their innocence. Kassin exemplifies this with the story of the witches' trial in Salem, US, in 1692, during which many innocent women were burned at the stake as a result of false admissions to witchcraft. Another example, closer to our times, is a rape case that occurred in New York in 1989 in which five young men admitted to being guilty following a prolonged investigation. They maintained that they were confident that if they admitted to being guilty, they would be released to their homes, but instead, they were formally charged and incarcerated. Only in 2002 were they released, when the real culprit was apprehended, admitted his culpability, and his admission was corroborated by a DNA examination. Third, false admissions by people who do not trust their memory and are convinced of their culpability. This phenomenon has been termed **memory distrust syndrome**, and Kassin has found a correlation between it and what has been termed **false memory**, observed sometimes in psychotherapeutic contexts. In both cases, an authoritative figure surfaces a unique insight from the subject's past that instills the subject with conviction regarding its authenticity. Kassin brings the example of the 14-year-old Michael Crowe, whose sister was stabbed to death. At the end of a prolonged investigation, during which he was presented with false physical evidence, he became convinced of having committed the crime claiming that he had not remembered how but he must have done it. He concluded that he must suffer from a split personality and that the "bad Michael" must have acted from jealous rage while the "good Michael" blocked out the incident. Ultimately, the charges against him were dropped when a vagabond was apprehended with the sister's blood smeared on his clothes. Kassin and his colleagues have helped release innocent suspects who have been indicted following their admissions and whose innocence was ultimately proved through DNA examinations which were not available during their trials (*The Innocence Project*).

The Canadian psychologist John J. Furedy and law professor John Liss demonstrate how it is possible without resorting to physical abuse or threats not only to convince suspects to take a polygraph test but also to convince them that they have committed a crime of which they are, in fact, innocent. They maintain that such incidents have led legal experts in Canada to oppose the use of polygraph in criminal contexts.

In Israel, it is impossible to forget the Amos Baraness case, for it provoked immense turmoil in the media and public at large and is considered as one of the more scandalous cases of false admission in the history of the country. Born in 1944, Baraness in 1976 was tried and convicted of the murder of Rahel Heller, a 19-year-old female soldier, who had been murdered 2 years previously. Baraness, who volunteered to help the investigation because he said he knew the victim, became the prime suspect in it, although the police had apprehended and interrogated other suspects as well. He was held in custody for a long time, during which he was deprived of sleep and subjected to severe physical pressure. Ultimately, he cracked and admitted culpability. Baraness was sentenced to life imprisonment, even though he recanted his admission claiming that it had been elicited through physical and psychological pressure. Upon serving 8 years of his sentence, he was pardoned by the president of Israel, following the disclosure of false police testimonies and other miscarriages of justice during his trial. Baraness did not settle for being pardoned and fought for a retrial, but in 2002, the state prosecutor decided not to indict him at all and to award him financial damages.

In an article that appeared in the most popular Israeli newspaper (*Yediot Ahronot*) in 1981, Ezra Goldberg, a retired police investigator, revealed to the journalist Eli Tavor, how the police investigation against Baraness had been conducted. Among other things, he revealed the report of the polygraph test results to which Baraness had been subjected in April 1975. The report, a photograph of which appears in the newspaper article, included the following questions: "Do you know who killed Rahel Heller"?; "Did you strangle Rahel Heller"?; "Did you meet with Rahel Heller on Wednesday, the 23rd of October"? The examiner's findings were formulated as follows: "… Most incriminating facts have been observed. We must express a reservation from a definitive determination, for it is our impression that the suspect suffers from psychological disturbances". The examiner's conclusion was formulated as follows:

> We believe that Amos Baraness murdered Rahel Heller. Because we have been impressed that the accused suffers from severe psychological disturbances, we were forced to express our reservation in the findings, but the nature of his psychological disturbance constitutes in our opinion a concurrent motive for committing the crime.

We do not see a real need to comment further on this conclusion, for it is so evidently groundless and grotesque. In fact, it could be positively funny had it not been so tragic. Since in Israel polygraph tests are not admissible in criminal court, the polygraph examiner's conclusion did not play a direct role in Baraness' conviction in court, but it is safe to assume that it influenced the police investigators who subsequently exerted pressure on Baraness to admit his guilt, and perhaps even influenced the state attorney.

The prevalent opinion today is that not only was Baraness not given a fair trial but that he was altogether innocent. Indeed, the reputable judge Haim Cohen, who chaired the Supreme Court when Baraness' appeal was rejected and he was sent to life imprisonment, not only changed his conviction in due course but also helped Baraness in his efforts to obtain a retrial.[3,4]

The directed lie test

The comparison questions used in the CQT are also referred to as "probable lie questions" because of the likelihood of the suspects to lie when replying to them. In recent years, a modification of the CQT called the Directed Lie Test (DLT) has been introduced. It is administered and scored in much the same way as the CQT. However, the DLT substitutes a directed lie for the probable lie comparison question. The directed lie is a statement that the examinee agrees to deliberately lie to, such as "Have you ever told even one lie"? or "Did you ever do anything that was illegal"? Examinees are told that this question provides an example of their reaction to a known lie and are instructed to think of a specific incident covered by their lie when they are asked the question. Several polygraph advocates have argued that because the DLT is more standardized than the CQT, it has the potential of being more accurate. However, several experimental attempts to compare the accuracies achieved by these two methods did not reveal significant differences.

The concealed information test (CIT)

Simultaneous to the development of the polygraph methods we have described above, which were elaborated mainly by field practitioners, an alternate polygraph method was developed, based on fundamentally different psychological principles, and on knowledge obtained from accumulative evidence-based psychophysiological research. The only common factor between this method and the ones described above is the use of the same physiological measurements. However, contrary to the methods described above, the Concealed Information Test (or in short, CIT), is not designated to detect deception directly but to determine whether the suspect possesses concealed **information**, information known to him only if he had been present at the crime scene. This is also why this method has been termed the CIT.

David Lykken, among the first psychologists to study the CIT, named it at the time the **Guilty Knowledge Test** (or in short, **GKT**). Obviously, this method may be applied only in cases of *event-related* detection of information.

In the CIT, the suspect is asked several multiple-choice questions, and each one of them is related to another aspect of the investigated crime/incident. For example, when a robbery has occurred, one of the questions may relate to the stolen item. The suspect is presented with several possible items, including the stolen one. If a gold watch has been stolen from a jewelry shop, the question relating to the stolen item will be "Have you stolen a gold watch"?, "Have you stolen a diamond bracelet"?, "Have you stolen the emerald earrings"? and so on. As a rule, it is advisable to present a minimum of five possibilities, including the relevant item. In this relatively simple method, even if the suspect is extremely nervous or aroused from the very test itself and apprehensive of its results, there is no reason why he would dread the relevant item more than the others and respond to it relatively more strongly. Therefore, if his response to the relevant item is stronger than to the other ones, it is reasonable to assume that the item is known to him. Naturally, a strong response to the concealed item in a single question is not sufficient, and so he is asked several questions of this type, and each one of them is repeated several times. When the suspect's responses to the concealed items in all the questions are consistently stronger, the examiner will conclude that he has knowledge of the concealed items. This situation is potentially incriminating unless the suspect manages to convince the investigators that he has obtained the information without being directly involved in the crime/incident. To illustrate this simple method, let us describe now a hypothetical situation as well as a suggestion to conduct a CIT in the context of an actual affair.

In the first example, our readers are requested to imagine the following event:

On April 26, 2018, at 2:00 a.m., the central safe of the First International Bank was robbed. It was situated on the ground floor of the bank. The sum of $1.2 million was stolen in six sacks; each one of them contained $200,000. The thief carried outside two sacks at a time, leaving their traces behind. He fled the scene in a stolen Honda Accord and forgot an empty bag of Cheetos in the safe. These facts were recorded by the security camera installed in a wall-clock whose purpose was to document every opening of the safe. Policemen arrested a suspect, and he was interrogated with the CIT. As a rule, each question relates to a separate category, and the concealed item is inserted among a few false items of the same category, known as neutral control items. Thus, our suspect may be asked the following questions:

1. Did you steal the sum of: 1 million, 1.2 million, 1.4 million, 1.8 million?
2. Did you flee the scene in: 1. a Nissan, a Toyota, a Ford, a Honda, a Chrysler?
3. Did you rob the bank at: 10 a.m., midnight, 2 a.m., 4 a.m., 6 a.m.?
4. Did you eat during the robbery: a chocolate bar, a potato chips pack, a bag of Cheetos, a doughnut?

Typically, the suspects are instructed to reply negatively to all the questions, but other procedures such as being silent or repeating the items' names are also possible. The suspect's physiological responses to the actual items are compared with his responses to the false items. A consistent measurement of stronger reactions to the actual items will bring the examiner to the conclusion that the suspect knows them. If the suspect's getaway car was indeed a Honda, then mention of the other cars constitutes control in the true sense of the word. A suspect who is involved in the robbery will have absolutely no reason to respond more strongly to the Honda even if he is terribly nervous and dreads the test result. He will be equally aroused by all the items. Indeed, ideally, it is advisable not to include in the questions items that are more threatening than others so that the only distinct feature of the relevant item is the fact that it is actually related to the crime scene. In addition, the concealment of the relevant items is, of course, crucial.

The second example we would like to present is related to an affair that actually took place in Israel, the John Demjanjuk affair. In 1988, Demjanjuk was tried and sentenced by a regional court in Jerusalem for crimes he had committed against Jews during the Second World War after he was identified by several Holocaust survivors as "Ivan the Terrible" from the Treblinka extermination camp. The defense argued that this was a matter of an erroneous identity and that he was in effect who he claimed to be. He was ultimately sentenced to capital punishment (which in Israel, as a rule, is very rarely practiced).[5]

Ironically, it was the prosecutor in the Demjanjuk trial who later on revealed some documents that could indeed call into question the identity of the suspect as Ivan the Terrible. Following the disclosure of these documents, the High Court reversed the sentence and proclaimed Demjanjuk "acquitted because of the benefit of doubt". Employing the CIT creatively in this case, as has been suggested by David Lykken, could have determined at an early stage of the trial whether Demjanjuk was Ivan the Terrible or not, for, as in every person's life, there were biographical facts engraved in his memory not known and not familiar to others. For example, the school he attended, the name of a pet, the name of a nanny or childhood friend, a dangerous childhood disease from which he had suffered, and so on and so forth. It is safe to assume that an in-depth investigation into Ivan the Terrible's past could have revealed such facts. Had Demjanjuk been interrogated with the polygraph CIT, and he responded – for example – more strongly to his mother's maiden name compared to other names, it would have been possible to link the two identities. But had he responded equally to all the biographical details of Ivan the Terrible, his defense argument would have been independently reinforced. Acquittal by the regional court would have saved the State of Israel considerable time, money, and embarrassment.

From the above examples, it is evident that the CIT is applicable only in *event-related* cases. But despite the fact that this method is scientifically based, it is unfortunately rarely applied in Western countries. Only in Japan, has it become the standard polygraph test in criminal contexts, and it is accepted as evidence in criminal courts. Finally, we should point out that besides the fact that it is not always easy or possible to conceal the relevant items during an investigation (for information often finds a way of leaking), it is also not always possible, even in event-related incidents, to employ the CIT. For example, in a rape or sexual assault case, when the question is whether or not the sexual act was consensual, we have a situation of his word against hers, and there are no concealed items involved that could link that suspect to the crime.

The CQT versus the CIT – where is the scientific basis?

In this discussion, we shall compare the CIT only with the CQT, for the R/I method is so absurd that it does not merit serious consideration at all. Furthermore, it has been abandoned as an investigation test in event-related contexts. In this critical discussion, we aim to show our readers why the CIT is a method based on scientific principles while the CQT is pseudo-scientific.

Following are five flaws that characterize the CQT and negate its scientific basis. The very fact that this method is not scientific does not necessarily mean that it does not have any practical value, for there are many nonscientific methods employed in criminal investigations. Nevertheless, distinguishing between scientifically based methods and those based on impressions and intuition alone is crucial. It is particularly important when we consider that the CQT might one of these days become admissible in criminal courts, but it is also important to reveal and explain its limitations for the benefit of those who might wish to make use of it, as well as for the public at large.

1. **Lack of theoretical basis and of logical rationale.** Any technique or method derived from scientific principles must be essentially and fundamentally based on a theory that may be tested and validated. The standard definition in the psychological literature regarding test validation – which is applicable to any diagnostic tool, and was formulated by the

American psychologist Samuel Messick – is an overall evaluative judgment of the degree to which empirical evidence and theory support the adequacy and appropriateness of the interpretations and actions based on test scores. For example, in tests that measure cognitive abilities in order to detect highly gifted children, a high score on the test is interpreted as evidence that the child is indeed gifted and the psychologist's recommendation will be to include him in a framework suitable to such children. In this case, the **question** will be, to what extent do the research and the theory support the psychologist's interpretation and recommendation.

Insofar as the CQT is concerned, there is no theory whatsoever that could establish a connection between physiological responses and lying. The psychological research shows that the physiological responses measured by the polygraph may also reflect psychological situations that have absolutely nothing to do with the act of lying. For example, when we are faced with an unexpected stimulation, similar responses to the ones used in the polygraph tests may be measured. A cognitive effort may also evoke similar responses. Emotions such as fear, stress, and tension also activate the autonomic nervous system and produce the same responses measured by the polygraph and interpreted as deception. Clearly, any suspect under polygraph investigation – whether truthful or deceptive – is likely to respond more strongly to the questions directly relevant to the crime attributed to him than to the control questions.

Even if we renounce the pretense of detecting lies from physiological responses (indeed, many of the CQT followers today agree that this is not possible) and settle for a more modest aim, that is, the involvement of a suspect in a crime, we shall still need a theoretical basis, or at the very least, a logical rationale that would justify the polygraph examiners' decision rule. The main downfall of this rule stems from the nature of the comparison questions. From the term "control questions", one might infer that there is actual control here. However, actual control demands that all the factors be equivalent, outside of the one we are investigating (in this instance, the factor of involvement in the crime).

Accordingly, the comparison questions should be equivalent to the relevant ones in all their details, with only the relevant questions connecting the suspect to the crime. That is, from an innocent suspect's point of view, there should be no difference at all between the two types of questions. But there is no such control in the CQT. The relevant questions refer to the specific investigated crime (i.e., "Did you steal the camera from your shop"?) while the comparison ones refer to general crimes or misdemeanors in the suspect's past (i.e., "Have you stolen anything from anyone in the past 5 years"?). Clearly, these questions are not equivalent; furthermore, even an innocent suspect could easily distinguish a question directly related to the event from a general question referring to his past.

In this context, John Furedy presents a particularly impressive example: In 1984, a crossing guard suspected for sexually molesting a 4-year-old girl was given the CQT. The relevant question presented to him (he was a 74-year-old man with no criminal record and no history of any sexual abuse) was, "Did you lick X's vagina"?; the control question was, "Have you ever done anything you are ashamed of"? Naturally, the old man responded more strongly to the relevant question – who wouldn't? – but the polygraph examiner concluded that this pattern of responses clearly attested to the suspect's culpability.

The CQT proponents defend it with the claim that an experienced examiner is able, during the pretest interview he conducts with the suspect, to formulate the comparison questions in a way that will ensure that an innocent suspect dreads them more than the relevant ones, and that only a guilty suspect will dread the relevant questions more. Is this really so? How can we tell whether a more conspicuous response to the relevant question is truly the result of a good choice of the comparison question posed to a guilty suspect, or rather the result of a bad choice of the comparison question posed to the innocent suspect?

As mentioned, in order to surmount the non-equivalence between the relevant questions and the control ones, during the pretest, the polygraph examiner tries to blur the distinction between them. But the examiner's assumption that the innocent suspect will fear the comparison questions more because he is unaware of the decision rule is unfounded because detailed descriptions of the CQT that include an explanation of the decision rule are available to the public at large both in the relevant literature as well as online. And once the suspect becomes aware of the decision rule, he has no reason to fear the control questions, for, in fact, they work in his favor. Thus, an innocent suspect aware of the CQT's decision rule is likely to show stronger relative responses to the relevant questions and consequently will be found deceptive.

Several years ago, some concealed information in a police investigation leaked to the press. The police announced that all the staff, including senior officers, would be given a polygraph test. One of the officers, a polygraph examiner in his past and therefore well acquainted with the CQT and the relevant and comparison questions, contacted Gershon Ben-Shakhar with the following dilemma: on the one hand, being well aware of the role of the comparison questions, it was clear to him that he could not take the test; on the other, a refusal to take the test could implicate him. This story alone teaches us that the CQT is primarily based on defrauding the examinees.

Unfortunately, from all the psychological and the psychophysiological literature that is available to us, we know that outside the polygraphists' strong belief, the CQT is devoid of any rationale or scientific basis, nor is it very convincing in its internal logic. Moreover, many researchers have stipulated the danger that this method creates a bias against innocent suspects because they are likely to fear the relevant questions more. It also gives an upper hand to the dishonest suspects, for if we assume that the response to the comparison question may reflect the fact that the suspect's response is a lie or at least that he is unsure of his answer, then the measure of the response is directly conditional on the odds that his answer is deceptive. According to this logic, a dishonest suspect who is accustomed to lying, cheating, and being hurtful to his fellow human beings will respond more strongly to the comparison questions and be found innocent in the test. And what have the polygraph examiners done following the harsh and steady criticism expressed – mainly by academic researchers – against the CQT? They changed its name. No longer is it the Control Question Test, but the Comparison Question Test. As if substituting the term "control" with the term "comparison" exempts us from the necessity to have actual control, which is the sole insurance we may have to protect the innocent from false incriminations.

In contrast, the CIT has a theoretical basis as well as a logical rationale. As we pointed out, it has no pretense of distinguishing between truth speakers and liars, but just detecting whether the suspect possesses any information that links him to the crime scene. This method does not depend at all on the verbal responses to the questions, and it is employable even if/when the suspects do not provide verbal answers. The psychophysiological literature on this topic is extensive and it includes scientifically validated theories that link the concealed information to the physiological responses measured by the polygraph. In addition, the CIT is based on a logical rationale, for the control questions in this method constitute actual control. That is, from an innocent suspect's point of view, there is absolutely no difference between the various items presented in the question.

This is not to say that the CIT does not have its limitations. It is imperative to collect relevant conspicuous items from the crime scene and make sure that they remain concealed. The Japanese have accumulated over 50 years of experience with the CIT, and the police in Japan have found ways to keep the concealed items from being disclosed.[6]

2. **Lack of standardization.** The scientific literature on psychological tests shows that standardization is a basic requirement in every test. This is an imperative requirement, for it ensures that all the examinees experience exactly the same procedure. Only and only when this requirement is implemented, the scores and the evaluations extracted from the test are meaningful and then and only then can we compare the various people who have taken the exam. In short, standardization is indispensable to the reliability[7] of a test.

The CQT is nowhere near respecting this principle. The pretest interview conducted by the examiner, which is part and parcel of every CQT, and during which the examiner formulates the comparison questions that constitute the basis of the CQT deduction process, is a totally subjective component. The choice of the comparison questions depends utterly on the examiner's intuition and on the relationship established between him and the examinee. The way the questions are presented to the examinee is also influenced accordingly; the examiner may, for instance, emphasize (i.e., by a change in his intonation, the intensity of his voice, his facial expressions, etc.) the relevant questions when he believes the suspect guilty, or emphasize the control questions when he believes the suspect innocent. Even some of the CQT followers agree on this crucial point. Because of the lack of standardization, the examiner's conclusion is more similar to that derived from an interview than from a standard objective test based on scientific principles.

In contrast, the CIT does not require any pretest interview. The questions are derived from the crime scene alone, and therefore, it is not necessary to tailor them for the suspects. In addition, it is not necessary that the person formulating the questions and the one presenting them during the investigation be one and the same. In fact, it is possible to conduct the CIT in a format similar to the one used in psychological experiments in which the experimenter is "blind" insofar as the relevant items are concerned, that is, he is ignorant of them. This format ensures protection from the examiner's judgment bias, as we shall see later on.

3. **Absence of objective quantification of physiological responses.** This is particularly astonishing, for the typical physiological measurements in the CQT may be easily quantified objectively using computerized methods. Objective quantification is a routine procedure in any psychophysiological experiment, and computerized algorithms have also been developed for physiological measurements in the CQT. Nevertheless, the majority of CQT polygraphists do not make use of these algorithms. There are polygraph agencies that rely on a general evaluation of the test charts (**the global method**, mentioned at

the beginning of this chapter). Clearly, this also renders the CQT impressionable and subjective, which in turn lends it extremely vulnerable to judgment bias, such as the confirmation bias (on which we elaborate in the next chapter). Other agencies use the analysis methods elaborated by Cleve Backster (the zone of comparison, described in the CQT review). Even though Backster's method constitutes a vast improvement over the global one, it remains subjective, because the assertion that the difference in the responses to a pair of questions (a relevant and a comparison one) is small, medium, or strong, is also subjective and therefore vulnerable to judgment bias.

There is no reason not to employ computerized algorithms for the CIT either, as is the norm in psychophysiological experiments. But even in Japan, where it is the standard polygraph test, such algorithms are not employed.

4. **Use of countermeasures.** In section (1) dealing with the lack of theoretical basis and of logical rationale, we showed how the CQT results and conclusions may lead to the incrimination of an innocent (or truthful) suspect who may appear deceptive as a result of the lack of equivalence between the relevant questions and the control ones. Here we shall show that there is also a danger in the opposite direction, namely, a bias that will cause the examiner to believe a guilty suspect innocent. Many experiments show that it is easily possible to train guilty suspects for a polygraph examination so that they would be found, with a high probability, innocent (or truthful). This necessitates adopting fairly simple techniques through which it is possible to heighten the responses to the comparison questions. Even if it is difficult to train people to avoid responding to the relevant questions, because the polygraphists' decision rule is based on a **comparison** between the responses to the relevant and the comparison questions, it suffices to heighten the responses to the comparison questions in order to make the examiner believe in the suspect's truthfulness. Responses to the control questions may be heightened either through physical means – such as tongue-biting – or through mental ones – such as thinking about a terrifying or arousing event, or mental activity that requires effort each time a comparison question is posed.

For all that, the American psychologist Charles R. Hont, who is among the CQT advocates, has shown that the use of countermeasures may have a very strong effect. In various experiments conducted by Hont and his colleagues, they found that the percentage of guilty examinees found truthful as a result of using countermeasures ranged between 50% and 70%. The use of countermeasures, or in other words, "cheating the lie detector", is not a downfall limited only to the CQT. The CIT is not immune to it either, as has been demonstrated by several experiments. Of late, the American psychologist Peter J. Rosenfeld and his colleagues have developed a method based on measurement of brain waves that could overcome the countermeasures against the CIT.[8]

5. **Contamination**. CQT polygraphists believe that it is vital that the same person formulate the relevant and comparison questions during the pretest interview as well as administer the test itself. The same person is also usually the one to analyze the test charts. As we pointed out before, the examiner also has access to the police investigation file. Moreover, during the pretest interview as well as during the test itself, the examiner may observe the suspect's behavior through and through and not just the physiological responses. Hence, the examiner knows more than the polygraph "knows". In other words, the examiner's evaluation and conclusion are based on more extensive knowledge than that elicited from the physiological channels themselves.

Hence, the knowledge available to the polygraphist is liable to influence the final conclusion, which does not necessarily attest to the accuracy of the polygraph's registrations. This obscures the ruling, for we shall never know to what extent it relies on physiological responses (i.e., the lie detector) or on the examiner's previous knowledge as well as on his impressions of the suspect during the test. This problem – known as **contamination** – is a serious methodological flaw that may have disastrous legal ramifications. In an effort to impede the use of the CQT in criminal trials, the Israeli psychologists Gershon Ben-Shakhar, Maya Bar-Hillel, and Israel Lieblich demonstrated these hazards some time ago. The rationale is simple: in addition to the CQT being inaccurate, files of criminal suspects may include items that are not admissible in court – such as previous convictions, hearsay testimonies, and evidence elicited through illegal means. If we allow CQT examiners to testify in criminal trials, these inadmissible findings will enter the courtroom "through the back door".

This problem is also closely related to the **confirmation bias** problem – on which we shall elaborate in Chapter 5, which deals with belief. We shall now exemplify the contamination problem and how it may lead to confirmation bias through a rather amusing item that was broadcasted in 1986 in CBS' *60 Minutes* and covered the use of the CQT. The producers conducted a sort of experiment through one of CBS' subsidiaries in which four people were employed. They invited four polygraphists who were asked to test the four employees, who – they were told – were suspected of having stolen expensive filming equipment from the company's offices.[9] Each polygraphist was told that the theft was clearly an inside job, for there were no signs of a break-in. They were all requested to test the four employees; however, they had been told separately, "We think that X did it", and X was told to be someone else to each one of the polygraphists. No argument or rationale was provided to the polygraphists for the suspicion of every X. The four employees were aware of the fact that they were participating in an experiment and were even promised a $50 bonus if found truthful, but they were unaware that they had been incriminated. Each of the polygraphists gave the "suspects" a CQT, and each one unequivocally concluded that employee X (who in each case was suspected without any proof or evidence) was lying while the others were truthful!

Another example we would like to present refers to a civil case that occurred in Israel several years ago, in which a judge had to decide between two opposing versions. Having a difficult time deciding, he did what often judges do in civil courts and suggested that the two parties take a polygraph test (as we point out time and again, in Israel, polygraph tests are not admissible in criminal courts but in civil cases they are, provided that all parties involved give their consent). In such a situation it is next to impossible to refuse the test, for, besides the fact that typically all parties are oblivious to the problematics involved, a refusal would easily appear suspicious. The two parties were given a

CQT by the same polygraph examiner. The examiner concluded that party A – who was the first to be examined – was truthful. Now, once he established that, what could possibly be his conclusion already at this stage regarding the other party? Indeed, after examining party B, he concluded that he was deceitful. Party B's lawyers protested and asked Gershon Ben-Shakhar to provide an expert opinion regarding the CQT. Ben-Shakhar requested to examine the details pertinent to party B's CQT, which revealed the following picture. Remember Cleve Backster's zone of comparison in which the examiner assigns numerical scores to each pair of questions (relevant and control) to each one of the physiological channels? Well, it turned out that in our case the examiner used this method and wrote next to each pair of questions, in each one of the channels, a score that indicated the difference between the physiological responses to the relevant and the comparison question. But, in quite a few instances, the examiner erased his original score and replaced it. At first glance, we could conclude that these alterations may have expressed some of the examiner's hesitations regarding the intensity of the responses to the relevant versus the comparison questions. But a closer look revealed that *all* the alterations, without exception, were made in favor of the examiner's initial assumption, namely that the party was deceitful. In other words, he had altered his evaluation of the physiological responses to match his early expectations. It is important here to stress that had it not been for the examiner's alterations of his initial scores, he could have not reached the conclusion he did. Even if he altered the scores unconsciously, or in good conscience, this does not validate his end result. Ultimately, the judge disqualified the procedure's findings, but, unfortunately, this example and many more like it have not diminished the popularity of the polygraph CQT in civil courts (and in the US in criminal courts as well).

The above two examples show how detrimental the contamination problem may be. In addition, the second example points to a more general fallacy common not just in polygraph tests. Had the judge been aware of the basic scientific principles employed in the social sciences, he would have refrained in the first place from referring the parties to the same polygraphist. His assumption must have been that the polygraph tests are not only scientifically based but also totally accurate. Hence, he was not aware of the possibility that had the two parties been examined by two independent polygraphists, they might have been both found truthful (or deceitful)!

As opposed to this, the CIT, as we demonstrated in the first section of this chapter, may be conducted from beginning to end "blindly". That is, the examiner himself – who presents the questions to the examinee – does not need to be aware of the relevant item in each question. The same goes for the person who analyzes the test results. This procedure necessarily ensures the elimination of the contamination factor and its emanative bias.

The replacement of the CQT by the more standardized DLT does not solve the problems described above. For both the CQT and DLT, the psychological impact of the comparison question is not equivalent to that of the accusatory relevant question, leaving both formats vulnerable to false-positive outcomes. Both methods are contaminated and prone to the confirmation bias. A naïve examinee taking a CQT may not realize that it is advantageous to augment the response to the comparison questions, but it is obvious that a strong response to the directed lie question is desirable, making it easier to understand how to use countermeasures with this format. The examinee is left to pick a lie of his choosing, and the examiner has no way of knowing how serious the transgression covered by the lie is. The more serious the lie, the greater the likelihood of passing the test. Criminals whose directed lies cover past undetected crimes they have committed may be especially likely to pass the DLT.

Accuracy of the CQT versus the CIT

At this point, our readers might rightly wonder about the accuracy rates or error rates in the methods we have reviewed. Seemingly, this is an empirical question that can be tested through research and experimentation, the results of which – if they indicate a high accuracy rate in the CQT – will render our criticism of it irrelevant. Regrettably, the actual reality of it is extremely complicated. All the research conducted to date has not been able to provide us with a simple straightforward answer concerning the accuracy rates of either one of the methods. We shall now review the reasons for it.

In order to be able to draw definitive conclusions from research results regarding polygraph tests conducted under actual circumstances, the research requires four fundamental conditions: (1) a clear unequivocal criterion regarding the examinees' (persons participating in the experiment) guilt or innocence. In the absence of such a criterion, we are clearly not able to determine whether the examiner's conclusion is right or wrong; (2) the criterion independent of the polygraphist's examination and the information available to him; (3) a statistical sample of the examined population and the cases for which polygraph tests are required; and (4) the conditions of the experiment similar to the ones in reality – in particular, the examinees must fear the test results and so take it seriously, and the lie or crime must be real.

Reviewing the scientific literature on the CQT validity reveals that not a single study exists today that has complied with the above conditions. In particular, there are no experiments that comply with the first and the fourth criterion concurrently. In 1982, a unique experiment was conducted and published, attempting to employ these four principles. The experiment included 21 Israeli police cadets who were given a series of psychometric exams. They were told that the exams' results would be taken into consideration in their future professional careers. In one of the exams, the examinees had to solve 25 logic problems. Upon completion of this section – for which no sufficient time was allocated – the hidden carbon paper that contained the examinees' initial answers was torn out, and the examinees were asked to score their own tests on a separate sheet. Thus, by comparing the carbon paper with the self-assigned scores, it was easy to tell who had forged his score by adding correct answers. It turned out that seven cadets had improved their scores. Several days later, the examinees were told that a suspicion of forgery had arisen, and they were advised to take a polygraph test in order to clear their names. They were told that their professional future depended on it. This experiment complies with the first condition, for the researchers knew with certainty who the cheaters were, as well as with the fourth, for the research was conducted under conditions very similar to actual conditions – the lie was authentic and the end result of the polygraph test would have real repercussions for the cadets. Similarly, the polygraph test results were independent of the examinees' culpability or innocence. However, as reality goes, two of the cheaters refused to take the polygraph test, another one who had agreed to take it did not show up, and three of the forgers admitted to the forgery prior to taking the test. Ultimately, there were 15 examinees left, out of whom only two had forged their scores. Clearly, no conclusion can be inferred from this sample. Moreover, such an experiment is not without its ethical problems, and so it is not surprising that the professional literature does not provide us with further similar studies.

All the studies complying with the first condition are mock studies (simulations) – in which the examinees are aware of participating in an experiment and of the role-playing. Some of the examinees (the "guilty" ones) are asked by the experimenter to "steal" an envelope containing money or some other valuable object. During the second stage, all the examinees ("guilty" and "innocent" alike) are tested by the polygraph examiner. They are asked by him to conceal their connection to the mock crime. At the end of the experiment, the examinees are thanked, remunerated, and sent on their way. Clearly, these conditions are in no way similar to real actual ones. Even though the first condition exists, for we know exactly who the guilty examinees are, the fourth condition is totally absent, for neither the "guilty" nor the "innocent" examinees fear the test results.

In another type of experiment, known as "field studies", employed in the CQT, actual crime files are employed, but only cases in which the truth is known by the suspects' admissions of the crime are sampled. Even if we overlook the possibility that the suspect's admission may be false, the sample is biased, since there might be a causal connection between the polygraph test results and the admissions, and this is a critical problem. This is because CQTs are used not only to reveal the truth but also as an investigative tool and as a means to pressure suspects into admission. Clearly, there exists a higher probability that a polygraphist will attempt to attain an admission from a suspect that shows "signs of lying" in his physiological responses than from one who does not demonstrate such signs. Thus, the admissions sample may include an overrepresentation of cases in which "signs of guilt" are recorded and an under-representation of errors.

This bias was excellently demonstrated by the American psychologist William J. Iacono, who showed that in principle, it is possible to obtain a 90% rate of accuracy in a sample based on suspects' admissions even when the actual accuracy of the polygraph test does not exceed the accuracy that is obtained by chance.

The research literature of the CIT is based on mock crimes as well (i.e., it is conducted under simulated conditions). Therefore, inferring conclusions from it in real-life situations is also problematic. There exists, however, a great difference: since in the CIT we compare the examinees' physiological responses to absolutely equivalent items (i.e., several types of weapons among which only one is the crime weapon), the examinees' apprehensions do not bear any influence on the results. Even if an examinee is extremely apprehensive from the test and its results, he has no reason to respond more strongly to the relevant item if he is innocent. Therefore, a generalization drawn from a mock CIT is more reasonable than one drawn from a mock CQT.

In view of the criticism we have presented regarding the CQT, it is not surprising that its results do not constitute admissible evidence in Israeli criminal courts. In 1978, the Minister of Justice appointed an investigative committee headed by the Supreme Court Judge Yitzhak Cohen to look into the polygraph applications, in particular, into the possibility of using the polygraph test results as evidence in criminal trials. The committee ruled for the interdiction of this possibility, stating among other arguments, that

> It would be dangerous that in this matter, in which doubt exceeds certainty, Israel will be perhaps the first country in the world, to allow limitless usage of the polygraph in legal procedures, as well as in pseudo-legal procedures that are not conducted in legal courts but involve critical decisions regarding a person's rights, in particular his/her freedom, honor, or property.[10]

The use of the polygraph in screening and classification processes

As we have seen, the polygraph was born and developed in the attempt to diagnose deceit and involvement of suspects in specific events. From the illusion that this aim has been accomplished by the lie detector (the CQT), rapid was the way to the idea that this machine may also distinguish between generally honest and dishonest people. Indeed, this idea led to the use of new polygraph practices whose aim is to select candidates for highly sensitive positions (e.g., industrial, security, and financial contexts), as well as to periodically test the loyalty and compatibility of employees in such functions. This is the non-event-related use of the polygraph. If we have managed in succeeding to convince our readers of the CQT's lack of any scientific foundation – and we hope we have – they will understand at once that even if the CQT had been able to provide valid evidence as to the suspects' innocence or guilt in regard to a specific event, the idea that it could provide us with reliable information regarding general human characteristics, unrelated to a specific event, is expressly fallacious.

Exams designated for classifying and screening personnel are meant to predict the candidates' behavior. In contrast to relatively constant human attributes, such as intelligence, attributes such as honesty, impartiality, integrity, and so on, depend on particular incidents and contexts (this issue was discussed at length in Chapter 3 on graphology). There is absolutely no evidence to show that a person who lied in one context or on one occasion will always lie or that a person who was once truthful will act the same in future incidences.

When the CQT is administered in screening contexts, the examinees are asked questions that refer to general and hypothetical misdemeanors, such as "Have you ever used drugs"? "Have you ever stolen from a previous employer"? and "Have you ever been accused of sexual harassment"?. We remind our readers that this type of question constitutes the control (or comparison) question in the CQT when a specific event is being investigated. But now that the control questions have become the relevant ones, what will the control questions be? Indeed, in the CQT screening process, there are no control questions in the acceptable sense – there cannot be such questions – and the conclusion is drawn from comparing the responses to the various relevant questions. If the examinee's response to the question involving drugs is stronger than his response to the other questions, the examiner infers that he has lied. This decision rule, in fact, brings us back to the two simplistic assumptions: that the physiological responses in the polygraph test reflect lies (the effect of Pinocchio's nose), and as we have demonstrated time and again, this assumption is totally unfounded; and that the truthful examinees will respond equally to all the questions. The latter is not only totally unfounded as well but is also totally illogical or irrational, for different people may indeed be aroused or perturbed differently by different issues in question. Some will be more perturbed than others – whether they are truthful or deceitful – by questions relating to sex than by questions related to theft, and vice versa.

During the 1970s and 1980s, the use of the polygraph for screening and classification prospered in the US and led to a very lucrative business. In 1988, following criticism and protestation, including from those who advocated the use of the CQT in specific events, the Congress enacted the Employee Polygraph Protection Act (EPPA), which banned the use of the polygraph in these contexts. However, this bill was applicable to the private sectors only and did not include government agencies related to issues of state security and law enforcement. The truth is that the use of the polygraph in screening and classification in the US is still quite prevalent. Candidates for highly classified positions are required to take such a test when applying, and personnel occupying such positions are required to take them periodically, notwithstanding the accumulation of positive as well as negative errors (missing "culprits" on the one hand, and false incriminations on the other). For years, a former American CIA agent Aldrich Ames sold to the Soviet KGB secret information because he managed to outsmart the polygraph in all the routine examinations he was given! In contrast, David Lykken brings the story of a Sovietologist who worked as a translator of the conversations held on the "red line" during Reagan's administration, who was found deceitful in a routine polygraph examination and as a result was temporarily denied his security clearance. The polygraphist's conclusion was drawn following the translator's negative reply to the question, "Have you ever discussed secret information with an outside source"? Lykken learned of this case when the translator called him regarding the chapter in his book that demonstrates the possibility of outsmarting the polygraph. In another telephone conversation, the translator told Lykken that the hardest thing he experienced during the polygraph examination was maintaining an indifferent expression.

At the outset of the second millennium, scientists employed in the US Department of Energy protested against having to take periodical polygraph tests, which seemed to them both humiliating and redundant. Following their complaints, the US National Research Council set up a committee headed by Professor Stephen E. Fienberg of Carnegie Mellon University with the intent to review the scientific evidence on the polygraph in general, and the use of the polygraph in screening and classification contexts in particular. The committee included 14 senior scientists from all the relevant fields – psychology, psychophysiology, statistics and operations research, biology, and law – who had no connection to the polygraph profession or to the research community studying deception detection. Its conclusion regarding the use of the polygraph in screening and classification contexts was as follows:

> Polygraph testing yields an unacceptable choice for DOE employee security screening between too many loyal employees falsely judged deceptive and too many major security threats left undetected. Its accuracy in distinguishing actual or potential security violators from innocent test takers is insufficient to justify reliance on its use in employee security screening in federal agencies.
>
> (NRC, p. 6)

This quotation points to two closely related problems: (a) the degree of accuracy of these tests is very low; and (b) but even if the level of accuracy had been much higher, because the prevalence of people who pose a security risk in federal agencies (spies, for example) is quite scarce, the polygraph tests will inevitably yield unreasonable rates of false incriminations of loyal employees. The report demonstrates this through a hypothetical example: if we assume that among 10,000 federal agencies there are ten spies and that the accuracy rate of detecting spies with the polygraph is 80% – a much higher rate than the actual one attributed to it by the committee – in order to detect eight out of the ten, almost 2,000 honest employees will fail the test. Let us observe Table 4.1.

But even this report with all the hard and serious work that has gone into it has not had the power to diminish this distressing phenomenon by much. We assume that this is so because of the tremendous power possessed by the federal agencies and the tests' power of deterrence in general, by virtue of their very existence and not by virtue of their inherent value, as our readers by now must have concluded themselves. As the American psychologists Harold Sigall and Edward Jones demonstrated in 1971 through an investigative method they named "the bogus pipeline", the very presence of a tool that does not have any function at all but is referred to as "lie detector", incented the examinees to respond with more honesty than in a situation in which they were not connected to any machine.

To sum up, in this chapter, we have reviewed the two major interrogative methods, based on psychophysiological measures:

1. The CQT (control or comparison), which is not necessarily event-related. We hope that we have succeeded in convincing our readers that this method has absolutely no scientifically based validity and that it is vulnerable to various biases. Because of these biases, guilty suspects may be found innocent with high probability while innocent and truthful ones may be found guilty.
2. The CIT, which is designed to diagnose concealed information and not lies or deceit and is necessarily event-related. Therefore, its use is limited only to situations in which the involvement

Table 4.1 A hypothetical example of attempting to detect a rare event

	Spies	*Non-spies*	*Total*
Detected as "spies"	8	1,998	2,006
Detected as "non-spies"	2	7,992	7,994
Total	10	9,990	10,000

Source: NRC (2003, p. 48).

of the suspects in a specific case is being investigated. It is based on scientific principles and uses proper controls. It is our recommendation therefore not to use the CQT at all and restrict the use of the polygraph to the CIT whenever possible. Against those who claim that the CIT is not practical because it is confined to specific events, we refer our readers to an analogy drawn by William Iacono between the CIT and fingerprints obtained from a crime scene, which are admissible as evidence in courts of law: even if we do not obtain fingerprints from every crime scene, no one would ever imagine doubting the fact that they constitute incriminating evidence whenever obtained. Similarly, evidence obtained from concealed items may be incriminating evidence, whenever it exists.

In the last decade, following the development of technological means enabling brain imaging, a new widespread line of research (using the fMRI) has emerged in psychology that attempts to describe the brain mechanisms that activate psychological processes such as perception, memory, attention, and learning. Attempts have been also made to detect the specific areas of the brain that are activated when we lie. This line of research has rekindled the yearning for a wondrous machine that could distinguish liars from truth speakers. The internet site of a commercial company called No Lie MRI, Inc. promises to deliver totally unbiased methods for diagnosing lies, and that this technology is the first one in our history to represent the only direct measurement for ascertaining deceit versus truthfulness. Rings a bell? Indeed, the attempt to diagnose lies through brain imaging is not essentially different from the attempt to diagnose lies through other physiological responses. Our enthusiasm with new technological inventions blinds us to the fact that the problem does not lie at all with finding a new diagnostic measurement but rather with finding a method that could overcome the acute problems we have described while reviewing the CQT. These are problems inherent in any attempt to detect lies directly. A series of scholarly articles published in 2009, severely criticized the use of fMRI for lie detection.[11]

The use of integrity tests as an alternative to the CQT

Following the 1988 EPPA passed by the US Congress, which prevents the use of lie detectors in the private sector for pre-employment screening as well as during the course of employment, employers began to seek alternative tests designed to predict future employees' honesty and integrity in order to minimize the risks of thefts and other counterproductive work behaviors (CWB). To this end, several paper-and-pencil integrity tests have been developed. Currently, integrity tests are administered by an estimated 6,000 US organizations and taken by as many as 5 million people each year.

Integrity tests are all self-report measures that can take two main forms: overt and personality-based measures. The overt tests are clear in their purpose and ask individuals directly about theft or CWBs. These direct questions can be framed as *attitudes* or *admissions*. For example, in the Personnel Selection Inventory (PSI, published by London House Press, 1980), we can find questions such as "How often in recent years have you thought about taking money without actually doing it"? (*admission*) and "A young person was caught stealing $50 in cash from an employer. If you were his employer, what would you do"? (*attitude*). Personality-based integrity tests, on the other hand, are not clear on their purpose and are similar to other personality tests in their structure. They may be thought of as attesting to various personality traits related to integrity, such as conscientiousness. Although conscientiousness and integrity are not the same construct, research has shown that conscientiousness is related to both types of integrity measures. Conscientiousness is typically assessed by the Big Five Personality Inventory (BFI), which measures the five major personality factors and has been used extensively in personality and individual differences research. The importance of measuring integrity is perhaps best demonstrated by the addition of a sixth factor to the BFI labeled "honesty-humility" that resulted in a new personality test – HEXACO.

Despite the popularity of integrity tests among employers and the fact that meta-analytic studies revealed that they can predict work-related criteria (e.g., job performance), these tests have remained controversial. They have been criticized mainly because of their vulnerability to faking and coaching. It would be naïve to expect someone who is applying for a job in a financial or security institution to admit to thinking about stealing money. In addition, many applicants for selective jobs are coached before applying and before taking admission tests. Because integrity tests' items, particularly overt tests, are completely transparent, coaching becomes easier and may severely bias test results. Indeed, research has demonstrated that overt integrity tests are affected by faking and even more by coaching. Instructing examinees to fake on such tests resulted in a significantly more favorable test outcome. Personality-based integrity tests are relatively unaffected by both faking and coaching. An additional critique of the use of integrity tests for job admissions is related to the high rates of false-positive decisions that may occur if job applicants are rejected based on the results of these tests. Such high rates are expected if the base rate of counterproductive behavior is low. We raised this issue when we discussed the use of the polygraph for personnel selection and in particular for screening employees who might turn out to be security risks. We demonstrated that even if polygraph accuracy rates are high (which we seriously doubt), their use for screening security risks will result in an intolerable rate of false-positive outcomes. Estimating the base rate of counterproductive behavior is rather difficult, and various researchers varied considerably in their estimates, which ranged from 5% to 60%. In 2007, the American Professors of Management Roland Karren and Larry Zacharias published a critical review of integrity tests, and, among other issues, they presented an analysis of the expected false-positive rates that would result if integrity tests were used to classify individuals as dishonest. Their analysis was based on the three estimates of test predictive validity (0.15, 0.30, and 0.40)[12] and on three estimates of base rates for theft (0.05, 0.35, and 0.60). These estimates yielded expected false-positive rates ranging from 50% (when validity is 0.40 and base rate is 0.65) to 99% (when validity is only 0.15 and base rate is 5%). When considering more realistic estimates of validity (0.30) and base rates (0.35), the expected false-positive rate is above 80%. Clearly, labeling 80% of job applicants as dishonest is quite alarming.

To conclude this section, we can confidently state, based on the vast literature on integrity tests, that they are better suited as a tool for personnel selection than polygraph tests. However, their use should be made with caution (i.e., in combination with other measures), and it is clear that personality-based measures should be preferred over the overt tests because they have larger validity estimates and are less affected by faking and coaching.

Perhaps it is no accident that humanity has not as yet invented a machine that distinguishes deceivers from truth-tellers or honest from dishonest people. We believe that the question whether we, as complex human beings operating in very complex social structures, truly desire such a machine, is not without ambiguity. Following is a joke that demonstrates this dilemma in a rather amusing way:

> A man returns to his home with a lie-detecting robot. His 12-year old son returns from school two hours later than usual.
> "Where have you been"? demands the father.
> "In the library, doing my homework", replies the son.
> The robot goes to the boy and slaps his face. The father explains: "This robot is a lie detector, you'd better tell the truth"!
> "Okay, I was at a friend's house, we watched the movie *The Ten Commandments*".
> The robot slaps the boy's face again and the father proclaims angrily: "Shame on you, when I was your age I never lied to my parents"! This time the robot slaps the father's face. The amused mother remarks: "Well, that's your son, alright"!, and it is, of course, her turn to be slapped by the robot!

Notes

1 The title of Lykken's book is taken from an essay published by the English author Daniel Defoe in 1730 in which he suggested that checking the pulse of suspected criminals may attest to their culpability or innocence.
2 In 2012, the *International Journal of Psychology* published a comparative study conducted in the US and China on lies used by parents in child-rearing. See www.tandfonline.com ("Instrumental lying by parents in the US and China").
3 Details regarding the relationship that developed between Judge Cohen and Baraness are covered in a long article published in the

weekend supplement of the Israeli newspaper *Ha'aretz* on December 2, 2011.
4 For those interested, more examples of false admissions are provided by Wikipedia at https://en.wikipedia.org/wiki/False_confession.
5 In Israel, even though capital punishment is possible (but only in special cases), it was carried out only in the case of the Nazi Adolf Eichmann, who was apprehended in Argentina, tried for his war crimes against Jews, and executed (hanged) in Israel in 1962.
6 Nayakama's and Osugi's papers provide in-depth reviews on the use of the CIT in Japan (see the Bibliography).
7 The reliability of a test is the consistency measure of the test scores in repeated measurements (for example, when different examiners give the same people the same exam a number of times).
8 A detailed account of the Rosenfeld method is provided in his and his colleagues' paper (see the Bibliography).
9 The fourth polygraphist's test was not recorded due to a technical failure; therefore, the item itself included only three tests.
10 From the *Report of the Commission on Polygraph Inquiry* (in Hebrew), January 1981.
11 See the Bibliography, *Using Imaging to Identify Deceit: Scientific and Ethical Questions.*
12 An explanation of predictive validity is provided in Chapter 3, and footnote 8.

Bibliography

Backster, C. (1963). Polygraph professionalization through technique standardization. *Law and Order, 11*, 63–64.

Ben-Shakhar, G. (1991). Clinical judgment and decision making in CQT polygraphy: A comparison with other pseudoscientific applications in psychology. *Integrative Physiological and Behavioral Science, 26*, 232–240.

Ben-Shakhar, G. (2002). A critical review of the Control Questions Test (CQT). In: M. Kleiner (Ed.), *Handbook of Polygraph Testing*. San Diego, California & London, UK: Academic Press, 103–126.

Ben-Shakhar, G., Bar-Hillel, M., & Kremnitzer, M. (2002). Trial by polygraph: Reconsidering the use of the GKT in court. *Law and Human Behavior, 26*, 527–541.

Ben-Shakhar, G., Bar-Hillel, M., & Lieblich, I. (1986). Trial by polygraph: Scientific and juridical issues in lie detection. *Behavioral Science and the Law, 4*, 459–479.

Ben-Shakhar, G., & Furedy, J.J. (1990). *Theories and Applications in the Detections of Deception*. New York: Springer-Verlag.

Bizzi, E., Hyman, S.E., Raichle, M.E., Kanwisher, N., Phelps, E.A., Morse, S.J., et al. (2009). *Using Imaging to Identify Deceit*. Cambridge, MA: American Academy of Arts and Sciences.

Bond, C.F. Jr., & DePaulo, B.M. (2006). Accuracy of deception judgments. *Personality and Social Psychology Review, 10*, 214–234.

De Vries, R.E., Lee, K., & Ashton, M.C. (2008). The Dutch HEXACO Personality Inventory: Psychometric properties, self-other agreement, and relations with psychopathy among low and high acquaintanceship dyads. *Journal of Personality Assessment, 90*(2), 142–151.

Elaad, E. (2005). *The Psychology of Lying and Methods of Lie Detection* (in Hebrew). Ramat Gan, Israel: Bar Ilan University.

Furedy, J.J. (1996). The North American polygraph and psychophysiology: Disinterested, uninterested and interested perspectives. *International Journal of Psychophysiology, 21*, 97–105.

Furedy, J.J., & Liss, J. (1986). Countering confessions induced by the polygraph: Of confessional and psychological rubber hoses. *Criminal Law Quarterly, 1986-1987, 29*, 92–114.

Ginton, A., Daie, N., Elaad, E., & Ben-Shakhar, G. (1982). A method for evaluating the use of the polygraph in a real life situation. *Journal of Applied Psychology, 67*, 131–137.

Honts, C.R., Raskin, D.C., & Kircher, J.C. (1994). Mental and physical countermeasures reduce the accuracy of polygraph tests. *Journal of Applied Psychology, 79*, 252–259.

Iacono, W.G. (1991). Can we determine the accuracy of polygraph tests? In: J.R. Jennings, P.K. Ackles, & M.G.H. Coles (Eds.), *Advances in Psychophysiology, Volume 4*. Greenwich, CT: JAI Press.

Iacono, W.I. (2011). Encouraging the use of the guilty knowledge test (GKT): What the GKT has to offer law enforcement. In: B. Verschuere, G. Ben-Shakhar, & E. Meijer (Eds.), *Memory Detection: Theory and Application of the Concealed Information Test*. Cambridge, UK: Cambridge University Press, 12–23.

Jones, E.E., & Sigall, H. (1971). The bogus pipeline: A new paradigm for measuring affect and attitude. *Psychological Bulletin, 76*, 349–364.

Karren, R.J., & Zacharias, L. (2007). Integrity tests: Critical issues. *Human Resource Management Review, 17*, 221–234.

Kassin, S.M. (2008). The psychology of confessions. *Annual Review of Law and Social Science, 4*, 193–217.

Kassin, S.M., Goldstein, C.C., & Savitsky, K. (2003). Behavioral confirmation in the interrogation room: On the dangers of presuming guilt. *Law and Human Behavior, 27*, 187–203. doi:10.1023/A:1022599230598.

Kassin, S.M., & Gudjonsson, G.H. (2004). The psychology of confession: A review of the literature and issues. *Psychological Science in the Public Interest, 5*, 33–67.

Larson, J.A. (1932). *Lying and Its Detection: A Study of Deception and Deception Tests*. Chicago, IL: University of Chicago Press.

Lee, K., & Ashton, M.C. (2004). Psychometric properties of the HEXACO personality inventory. *Multivariate Behavioral Research, 39*(2), 329–358.

Levine, T.R., Asada, K.J.K., & Park, H.S. (2006). The lying chicken and the gaze avoidant egg: Eye contact, deception, and causal order. *Southern Communication Journal, 71*, 401–411.

Lykken, D. (1998). *A Tremor in the Blood: Uses and Abuses of the Lie Detector*. New York: Plenum Trade.

Marston, W.M. (1938). *The Lie Detector Test*. New York: Smith.

McCrae, R.R., & Costa, P.T. (1987). Validation of the five-factor model of personality across instruments and observers. *Journal of Personality and Social Psychology, 52*, 81–90.

Meijer, E.H., Verschuere, B., Gamer, M., Merckelbach, H., & Ben-Shakhar, G. (2016). Deception detection with behavioral, autonomic and neural measures: Conceptual and methodological considerations that warrant modesty. *Psychophysiology, 53*, 593–604.

Messick, S. (1995). Validity of psychological assessment: Validation of inferences from persons' responses and performances as scientific inquiry into score meaning. *American Psychologist, 50*, 741–749.

Munsterberg, H. (1908). *On the Witness Stand*. New York: Doubleday.

Nakayama, M. (2002). Practical use of the concealed information test for criminal investigation in Japan. In: M. Kleiner (Ed.), *Handbook of Polygraph Testing*. San Diego, CA: Academic Press, 49–86.

National Research Council. (2003). *The Polygraph and Lie Detection*. Committee to review the scientific evidence on the Polygraph. Division of Behavioral and Social Sciences and Education. Washington, DC: The National Academies Press.

Osugi, A. (2011). Daily application of the CIT: Japan. In: B. Verschuere, G. Ben-Shakhar, & E. Meijer (Eds.), *Memory Detection: Theory and Application of the Concealed Information Test*. Cambridge, UK: Cambridge University Press, 253–275.

Reid, J.E. (1947). A revised questioning technique in lie-detection tests. *Journal of Criminal Law and Criminology, 37*, 542–547.

Reid, J.E., & Inbau, F.E. (1977). *Truth and Deception: The Polygraph ("Lie Detector") Technique* (2nd ed.). Baltimore, MD: Williams & Wilkins.

Rosenfeld, J.P., Labkovsky, E., Winograd, M., Lui, M.A., Vandenboom, C., & Chedid, E. (2008). The Complex Trial Protocol (CTP): A new countermeasure-resistant, accurate, P300-based method for detection of concealed information. *Psychophysiology, 45*, 906–919.

5

"Since man cannot live without miracles, he will provide himself with miracles of his own making"[1]
The belief in practices based on cold reading, mysticism, and pseudo-science

The need to believe

The need to believe is a fundamental human need. People – women, men, and children alike – need to lean on something because the notion of our lives being arbitrary is so hard to bear, because so many things in life are subject to chance and good fortune, because it is next to impossible to make sound decisions under uncertain conditions – which is the case in most circumstances – and, last but not least, because we are aware of our finality and our inability to prevent it.

Some of us believe in a Supreme Being and all its derivatives and follow positive and negative precepts without exception; some adopt dictates, life philosophies, and various spiritual beliefs; some have chosen not to believe in anything and, as a result, are continuously searching for answers, for believing for them is just as essential as for others. In fact, these might be the ones who will tend to stream along after anything that might impress them as reliable, particularly if they are promised to be furnished with the ultimate truth, and with knowledge regarding their future, whose obscurity instills in us the fear and trembling that is also the bread and butter of psychologists, psychoanalysts, and psychiatrists. The danger of producing false findings or evidence as a result of strong beliefs extends to scientists as well, and they are warned against it time and again. Keith Stanovich quotes Nobel Prize winner Peter Medawar regarding advice he gave scientists who tend to fall in love with their theories or hypotheses: "… the intensity of a conviction that a hypothesis is true has no bearing on whether it is true or not".

Moreover, we tend to believe especially in those things that are commonly believed in. Our assumption is that if so many people believe in something, there must be some truth in it. We also tend to believe that if a belief prevails long enough, it must be true. Lilienfeld and his colleagues see in this tendency a myth rooted in our inclination to swim with the tide. They term this phenomenon the Bandwagon Fallacy.

Abuse of the need to believe

All the practices we have reviewed in our book are snares that abuse the human need to believe, whether consciously and/or cynically whether unconsciously. Hence none of us is immune to them and sooner or later might fall into a trap of one kind or another. A well-known anecdote tells of Niels Bohr, the celebrated Danish Nobel Prize winner in Physics, who invited a few colleagues to his house. Upon arrival, they noticed a horseshoe hanging at the entrance door. Stunned by what they had just noticed, they asked how a distinguished scientist like Bohr believed in such foolish superstitions. "Of course, I don't", replied Bohr, "but they say that it helps even those who do not believe"! Whether this situation occurred in reality or not, it does demonstrate that even the most outstanding scientists, who as a rule do not believe in anything that is not evidence-based, are well aware of the complex human psychology.

Therefore, it is most important for us to emphasize that we honor and respect – and most of all, understand – people's need to have faith (how can we do without it?) and the various creeds. Our criticism is not directed at them, nor at faith per se – how can anything be achieved in this world if we do not have faith in ourselves and in our endeavors? – but solely at people or institutions who abuse our need to believe. Notwithstanding our sincere understanding, we do hope to bring our readers a little closer to the English scientist Rosalind Franklin's statement, "I maintain that faith in this world is perfectly possible without faith in another world".

Popular beliefs

Not once do we find ourselves engaged in a conversation in which someone mentions the findings of a research study from which we may learn something about the topic that has been scientifically investigated. But it suffices for someone to emit an utterance such as "… but I have a friend who …", or "I've done so and so during one year and it really helped", or "There was a long article about it in the Washington Post", and away fly the scientific findings, back to the ivory tower of academia, where they will find an open eye and an attentive ear only among those who share the same field. Time and again people will choose to believe in unfounded opinions rather than in knowledge produced by systematic scientific investigation.

As we have already pointed out, most of us find it difficult, or even impossible, to follow up on scientific findings, for we most certainly lack the tools for it. In contrast, our ability to fully participate in anecdotal information has the power to create the illusion that we have been given easy access to "the facts".

In his book, Keith Stanovich discusses, among other things, the problem of popular beliefs, and what is known as common sense, stressing that our thinking and behavioral patterns suffer from a lack of consistency and coherency that no scientific theory will allow itself. He demonstrates the inherently self-contradictory popular beliefs as reflected in popular, "sensible" proverbs. "Look before you leap" has a relative in "He who hesitates is lost"; "Absence makes the heart grow fonder" may become in different circumstances "Out of sight out of mind"; if "Haste makes waste", why does "Time wait for no one"? How could the saying "Two heads are better than one" not be true? Well, because we also have the "sensible" proverb, "Too many cooks spoil the broth"! And if we believe that "It's better to be safe than sorry", then what about "Nothing ventured nothing gained"? If "Opposites attract", why do "Birds of a feather flock together"? Stanovich admits that he himself has counseled many students to "Never put off until tomorrow what you can do today", as well as to "Cross that bridge when you come to it". Do we adapt our beliefs according to our heart's desires, to the concrete circumstances of our lives, and to our moods? In this chapter, we attempt to analyze these questions in depth.

Bias in human judgment

Why do intelligent people believe in completely unfounded practices? This complex question has, as expected, more than one answer, and most answers are related to the fact that human judgment is vulnerable to many prejudices. In their discussion of human judgment, G.A. Dean and his colleagues[2] quote William Shakespeare, who in 1600 gave his protagonist Hamlet one of the most famous soliloquies regarding human nature:

> What a piece of work is man! How noble in reason! How infinite in faculties! In form and moving, how express and admirable! In action, how like an angel! In apprehension, how like a god! The beauty of the world! The paragon of animals!
>
> (Hamlet, act 2, scene 2)

In the context of the play, this soliloquy is deeply ironic, an irony ignored by Dean and his colleagues in their context for the purpose of making their argument. They proceed to quote the Nobel Prize winner in Economics in the year 1978, Herbert Simon, who made the following statement three centuries later (1957):

> The capacity of the human mind for formulating and solving complex problems is very small compared with the size of problems whose solution is required for objectively rational behavior in the real world – or even for a reasonable approximation to such objective rationality.

On these two opposing views, the authors quote J.S. Armstrong:

> On almost any basis one would choose Shakespeare! He is more poetic than Simon; more widely read; and his position is more popular. The only thing that Simon has going for him is that he is right.

Had the authors taken into account Shakespeare's irony, perhaps they would have refrained from drawing this comparison, for it would have meant that Shakespeare and Simon are indeed of the same opinion, which would have meant that three centuries have not altered the human being's judgment by much! But do let us, for argument's sake, comply with them and accept Shakespeare's words at face value.

Indeed, the human behavior reflects Armstrong's statement. This assertion is supported by a rich body of experiments initiated by Amos Tversky and Daniel Kahneman[3] in the 1970s. These experiments focused on decision-making and judgment under uncertain conditions and pointed to a series of judgment biases typical of these situations. In addition, the psychological research that examines decision and judgment processes shows that very often, we have a tendency to overtrust the accuracy of our judgment.[4]

One of the more common human biases is our tendency to find significance in things that have no significance at all. A good example of this is the illusory correlation, that is, the belief that there is a strong relationship between two variables, although in reality, they are slightly, or not at all, related. Moreover, we tend to assume that if two things occurred consecutively, then one must have influenced the other, that is, there must be a causal relationship between them. Illusory correlations may be found both in scientific experiments as well as in realistic situations.

Stereotypes and superstitions make a good example of illusory correlation. Studies show that we have a tendency to attribute certain personality traits to certain ethnic groups without any factual grounds (e.g., Jews love money, Arabs understand only power, the Italians are such thieves, Germans have no sense of humor, people in small towns are nice). The number of superstitions is infinite: starting with popular beliefs (e.g., crossing a black cat is bad luck), and ending with personal, individual superstitions. In this context, we cannot but think of Groucho Marx's famous – and particularly funny – statement, "If a black cat crosses your path, it signifies that the animal is going somewhere"!

Following is an example of a personal superstition reflecting illusory correlation. A student wears her watch on the wrong hand because she hastens to make it on time for an exam. She scores exceptionally well in her exam and her mind internalizes an illusory correlation between wearing her watch on the right hand and doing well on the exam. She internalizes this incident because it is irregular (in this case, positive, but similarly it could have been a negative incident). Strangely enough, all the times that our student has worn her watch on her left wrist and done well on her exams are not taken into account. Hence, her mind has recorded a correlation between wearing her watch on her right wrist and doing well on her exams. From now onward, she will always wear her watch on her right wrist during an exam. We may see how the illusory correlation is strongly linked to the way our memory records things.

In a series of studies conducted by the American psychologist Jane L. Risen and her colleagues in 2007, the experimenters showed that rare behaviors in people belonging to minority groups are perceived differently from common behaviors in people belonging to minority groups, as well as from both rare and common behaviors in people belonging to majority groups. For instance, they showed that one example of unusual behavior (e.g., violent behavior) on the part of someone who belongs to a minority group (e.g., Muslim) suffices to create an illusory correlation between that particular behavior and the ethnic ascription of the individual (i.e., Muslims are all violent).

Notwithstanding, there are psychologists who claim that given our human cognitive abilities, among which is our ability to symbolize and find meaning in various things, it is no wonder that we also attribute significance to things expressly devoid of significance. They claim that paradoxically, it is precisely our wisdom and our creativity that enable us to flee from rational thinking.

Our tendency to find meaning in meaningless things stems from the difficulty to live with the knowledge that the world is largely arbitrary, uncertain, and meaningless. This difficulty also accounts for our tendency to believe in the occult, in the next world, and in various cold readers. The famous Russian novelist Fyodor Dostoyevsky illustrates this point well in his *The Brothers Karamazov*:

> Since man cannot live without miracles, he will provide himself with miracles of his own making. He will believe in witchcraft and sorcery, even though he may otherwise be a heretic, an atheist, and a rebel.

Indeed, Dostoyevsky touches upon a common human need, and we will now attempt to explain the psychological reasons for its existence in relation to the practices we have reviewed while relating both to the clients' as well as to the suppliers' belief.

The clients' belief
The burden of doubt and incertitude

From all we have claimed until now, we may understand that the belief in irrational things and in unfounded practices stems from the fact that the primary, most important aim of human judgment is not precision but the elimination of doubt and incertitude, which have the power to paralyze us.

Our fright from incertitude instructs our judgment processes in a way that would enable us to make a decision without much hesitation and with a high level of certainty. People who "waste" time in decision-making – starting with shopping in supermarkets, through buying an apartment or investing their savings, and ending in choosing a life partner – are perceived as helpless and lacking in self-confidence. Indeed, as a rule, recurring hesitations are not the result of a rational procedure of decision-making. As we pointed out before, in our mundane lives, we have neither the tools nor the possibility of rationally weighing all the various alternatives facing us and the potential outcome of each alternative, and estimating their probability.

Let us examine the simple example of savings investments. The possibilities are numerous: the stock market, bonds, foreign currencies, real estate, and so on. Every decision holds in store future outcomes whose probabilities are very difficult – maybe even impossible – to estimate. The issue becomes even more complicated when the decision in question involves personal choices, such as the choice of a life partner.

Hence, should we run into someone who offers us a magic solution through one of the practices we have reviewed, a solution which may aid us in making a decision while minimizing the uncertainty and the burden accompanying it, it is not hard to understand how so many of us jump on the opportunity. In one of the articles that covered cold reading in the Israeli magazine *Lady Globes* mentioned in the chapter on cold reading, it is assessed:

> In a multi-million dollar, clandestine market, names of "witches" and "prophets" are being passed on from one another, as a particularly guarded secret. Behind the curtains, predictions and implantation of thoughts have become part and parcel of the portfolio in the negotiation of important deals, or in making critical personal decisions. More and more high executives in the Israeli economy, become dependent on secret, highly intuitive, councilors .... Business people, Jurists, Politicians, and intellectuals, are seeking behind the curtains advice from councilors who attribute to themselves extra-sensory powers.

So, important businesspeople are accustomed to taking counsel from various cold readers when they are faced with serious decisions regarding their businesses. The situation is similar in other fields we have surveyed. An employer who hesitates between two candidates that appear equally qualified will be happy to receive advice from a graphologist who will ultimately recommend the more suitable candidate after having examined both their handwriting. A judge who hesitates between opposed versions of two rivals appearing before him might suggest "the magic machine", that is the polygraph (the Comparison Question Test, CQT, common in Israel), and let it have the final rule.

The need to remove personal responsibility

Another hardship accompanying the human existence in this context is personal responsibility for the outcome of decisions that may prove (always in retrospect) wrong or unwise. This difficulty is well reflected in the amusing statement of the astrologists quoted in Chapter 1, "Not the astrologers have deceived us when they assured us that there was no immediate threat pending from the gulf area. The stars had deceived them, even though they won't admit it".

In the chapters that dealt with graphology and the polygraph, we have seen that the practice of them is very common in the context of personnel selection and evaluation. The personality trait that employers value the most, especially when highly sensitive functions are involved (state security, industrial confidentiality, and so on), is honesty. However, as we have explained, this is a human trait which is tremendously hard – or even impossible – to evaluate a priori. Hiring employees who will end up embezzling money or leak classified information will be perceived as a severe mistake on the part of the employers. Hence, transferring the responsibility onto "professionals" such as graphologists or polygraphists exonerates them at once.

In our personal lives, we tend to project responsibility onto others as well. The projective mechanism is almost infinite. Both in institutional hierarchies, as well as within our own families, we tend to put the blame on others when things do not turn out the way we hope or wish. Therefore, leaning on "experts" to tell us whether the positions of the stars is right for choosing a spouse or an apartment is most tempting, since it relieves us of the responsibility. Not only do we save ourselves precious time hesitating between the alternatives, we also save ourselves the guilty feelings that flood us when we realize that our decision has not been favorable to us. An Israeli psychiatrist states in *Lady Globes*,

> It is in the human nature to seek for an anchor. Their belief that there is a power higher than us, helps them to go on with their lives and reduce the stress, the worry and the fear in them. The idea that the responsibility and the control of

our lives rests in our hands – for better or for worse – is quite hard to bear, for there is no one to blame. And there is no one to turn to for making things better, it's all our responsibility.

The influence of the Barnum effect

We elaborated on the Barnum (or the Forer) effect in Chapter 1. We remind our readers that this effect refers to a very general personality description that may match each and every one of us. This kind of description constitutes a central tool for convincing clients of the validity of graphology and astrology. When a graphologist offers his services to a particular enterprise, he is not required to provide any scientific research data in support of the evaluations offered. Instead, the graphologist requires the potential client (e.g., the head of human resources of an enterprise) to provide him with handwritten examples. Their evaluations are usually Barnum evaluations, so that the clients are easily convinced of their efficiency.

Bias for positive evidence

Another very common human tendency is to lean toward positive suggestions and evaluations rather than toward negative ones, as well as to prefer the ones that flatter us. We will reiterate here one of Hyman's assertions that the Barnum effect works, among other reasons, when the stock spiel includes many more positive statements than negative, albeit a few negative statements are necessary in order to render the description credible.

We believe that most consumers of cold reading are people in distress, who have undergone trying periods or hardships, or are very unsure and frightened by their prospective future. In such circumstances, people are in dire need for consolation and encouragement, and for words to alleviate their pain. This is also the reason why they tend to cooperate with the cold readers who give them exactly what they need. In the chapter dealing with cold reading, we saw how these manipulations work on us like magic.

In addition, we tend to be captivated by positive, flattering statements regarding our personality, even when those are surprising and incompatible with what we know about ourselves. Imagine someone who has worked all his professional life in a dreary office being told by one reader or another, "You have enormous creative potential that has not been fulfilled yet, you are a sensitive person with very rich imagination". Who will not be happy to introduce such an exhilarating promise in his otherwise gray existence? It is indeed possible that some of us have unfulfilled potential (maybe even most of us) for, as complex human beings, we are endowed with abilities and virtues that are not always expressed. What is totally impossible and implausible is that someone should have the ability to detect all this in our handwriting, in the position of the stars, or in a bunch of Tarot cards.

We commonly tend not to interpret such statements as untrue, but on the contrary – our belief in the capacity of the expert to decipher wondrous personality traits unknown to us so far will increase. It is worth mentioning that this tendency is often what makes psychotherapy or psychoanalysis fail, for clients begin their therapy with the fallacious assumption that the therapists or analysts will soon place in their hands the key/secret to resolving all of their problems and materializing all of their dreams. In other words, the clients have an irrational expectation that their therapists will unlatch their innermost secrets and inhibitions with the wave of a hand. In reality, this is a lengthy process that requires much patience, dedication, and compliance on the part of the clients. But in conference with the "experts" we tackle here, we receive immediate advice and answers, that is, instant satisfaction.

Social and cultural influences (conformity)

All the practices we have reviewed have earned wide popularity in the various media. Newspapers and magazines publish daily, weekly, monthly, and yearly horoscopes. Radio and television channels broadcast daily programs in which the listeners and viewers may call the "experts" with any question at all, bare their hearts and souls, and receive at once a detailed response to their problems. The television broadcasts series such as Lie to Me and The Mentalist, in which protagonists endowed with superpowers

126 Belief in pseudo-scientific practices

help the police or other institutions solve crimes. In many detective series and many American films, the polygraph is suggested as a reliable tool for detecting lies and liars. In Israel, in almost every criminal affair, it is suggested time and again that suspects be submitted to a polygraph Control Question Test, even though its findings are not allowed as evidence in a criminal court.

All this publicizing affects us deeply, for our opinions and values are strengthened through conformity and through social and cultural norms prevailing in our environments. We stress this point, for most of us are unaware of our tendency for conformity, and we like to believe that we are independent thinkers who keep an open mind. The American psychologist Salomon Asch[5] demonstrated this tendency in the 1950s in a set of experiments he conducted. In one experiment, he invited 123 students to his lab and told them that the experiment seeks to examine how people perceive the length of lines. The participants were asked to evaluate the length of different lines as they appear in Figure 5.1.

Each participant was seated in a room with 4–6 "collaborators" (with Asch), who had been previously instructed how to react to each question. The participants were not aware of this fact and thought that the collaborators were participants like them. The experiment included 18 trials, and in each one of them, all the participants present in the room (including the collaborators) were asked to state out loud which of the three lines appearing in the right quadrate is identical to the one appearing in the left one. The collaborators were asked to give the wrong answer in 12 of

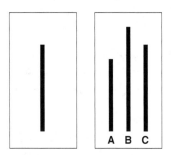

Figure 5.1 Description of the stimuli used in Asch's experiment.
Source: Asch (1951).

the trials. The real participant was always the last one. Asch's research question was simple: "Will the real participants display conformity, in that, will they follow the collaborators and give a wrong answer in the 12 trials"?

Indeed, the results of this experiment showed that a third of the participants gave wrong answers in the total number of trials and that 75% of the participants displayed conformity in at least one of the trials. At the end of the experiment, the participants who had displayed conformity were interviewed. Most of them claimed that they did not really believe in the answers they gave but decided to follow the group so that they would not be mocked by the others. Only a few admitted to believing that the answers they gave were correct.

Throughout the years this experiment has been numerously repeated, and many researchers examined the various factors that influence conforming behavior. One of the factors examined has been the degree of difficulty of the task. The findings showed that the more difficult the task is (that is, the more similar the lines are), the larger is the number of participants who display conformity. This is not surprising, for the lesser the confidence we have in ourselves, the more we tend to rely on the opinions of others.

Since the decisions we have to make in our real lives are infinitely more complex than having to decide on the lengths of lines, it is safe to assume that in real life, the tendency – the need – to conform is much greater. It is no surprise, therefore, that people are drawn into the practices we are discussing when these receive so much publicity in various media without being accompanied by any kind of control or criticism. The impression one gets, as a result, is that if they are so popular, they must be reliable.

We have brought Asch's experiment to demonstrate conformity, yet, we would like to point out one important distinction between Asch's participants and the clients of the practices we are discussing. Most of Asch's participants detected the differences in the length of the lines and still decided to go along with the majority decisions to avoid being subjected to mockery. But in real life, the clients of the practices discussed are not in the least aware of the mechanisms behind them and are totally ignorant of their degree of validity, or rather its absence. And if we may be tempted to go with the tide when we are aware of the fact that we are making a mistake, then, so much the more when we are not aware of it.

Shifting the burden of proof

The fundamental assumption of scientific thought is to call into question every single theory and to find evidence that supports it. In that, in science, the burden of proof regarding the validity of a theory (or a hypothesis) rests upon the researchers who suggest it.

However, our behavior in mundane life shows the polar opposite. In so many incidences, we tend to believe anyone who will offer us some magical merchandise (e.g., the polygraph), and in fact, expect the skeptics to provide the evidence for its lack of validity. In that, our fundamental assumption is that the practice offered by the suppliers is reliable unless it is otherwise proven. Let us examine this simple example: if X tells Y about the wonders of an astrologist, and Y displays skepticism regarding the possibility of learning about people from the position of the stars, it is X who will always expect Y to provide him with proof regarding his skepticism, or to provide an alternative explanation for the astrologist's success ("So explain to me how she knew that I was a creative person and have analytical talent"?). So, the question that always arises in these situations is that if the faith in astrology, or any other such practice, is totally unfounded, how may we account for the success of the practitioners? Not only does this attitude contradict scientific thought, but it is also totally irrational, for it is evident that the suppliers of the practices have the burden of proof regarding the reliability of their practices. Who has the obligation to prove that a certain device works, its seller or the buyer expressing doubt regarding its efficiency?

The practitioners' belief

No doubt, some of the practitioners we have described so far have chosen their practice for financial gain and do not necessarily believe in its validity. In other words, these are charlatans who knowingly deceive their clients and profit from their innocence. However, many other practitioners, perhaps even most of them, believe wholeheartedly in the validity of their practices. The latter not only deceive others but also themselves.

We wish to remind our readers of Ray Hyman's story from Chapter 2, who started believing in his ability to detect personality traits from palm reading until he found out that even when he read the lines of the palm contrary to what the lines "showed", he was not any less successful. In the article we mentioned from *Lady Globes*, numerous cold readers were interviewed who claimed to have supernatural powers, the ability to identify "energies" across time and place, and foresee the future. The faith of one of the readers brought her to state that "the future of the Israeli economy does not really depend on the financial experts but on the spiritual advisors who tell them what to do". This statement seems to us at best amusing and at worst most alarming. We will further demonstrate the practitioners' beliefs through an incident that occurred in Israel at the end of the 1970s. Classified information was leaked from a cabinet meeting in which senior ministers participated and, as is often the case in such circumstances, it was suggested that all the participants submit to a polygraph test. The incident was covered by popular media, and consequently, a senior polygraphist was invited to the only Israeli television channel that existed back then. He demonstrated how the device works, a thing that always impresses people because of the scientific aura that surrounds the measurement of physiological responses. After this, he was asked about the accuracy of the polygraph to which he replied that in the 1,500 tests that he had conducted, there was only one mistake! Now, this reply made, no doubt, a huge impression on the naïve viewers, but anyone with minimal knowledge of psychology, biology, or science, in general, knows that there is no device on earth with a level of precision that even comes close to this. Furthermore, as he did not have any independent information regarding the veracity of these 1,500 examinees, it is rather curious how he could have made such a strong statement. But the point we are trying to make is that the polygraphist actually believed in the data he gave. The disparity between the practitioners' belief in the accuracy of their devices and the lack of empirical supporting evidence may be explained by two main factors: one is the confirmation bias, and the other is illusory validity.

The confirmation bias

Researchers who have investigated the phenomenon known as confirmation bias explain it as a human tendency to look for or interpret evidence in a way that conforms to our prior expectations, our prior beliefs or our hypotheses. The British psychologist Jonathan Evans thinks that in all of the research that has been published in the area of human judgment, confirmation bias is probably the most salient example of judgment error. Following are a few examples of confirmation bias.

An experiment published in 1998, conducted by Gershon Ben-Shakhar and colleagues, examined confirmation bias in expert judgment. Expert clinical psychologists participated in it. They were given the results of a series of common psychodiagnostic tests (e.g., the Rorschach test) and were asked to analyze them and make a diagnostic evaluation. To half of the participants, it was suggested that the patient who had been tested may be suffering from a borderline disorder, and to the other half, it was suggested that the person who had been tested suffered from a paranoid personality disorder. Despite the fact that all the psychologists analyzed the same diagnostic tests (that did not refer to any specific person), their diagnostic evaluation matched the initial suggestions regardless of what the tests showed. The American psychologist Timothy Levine and his colleagues conducted an experiment whose findings were published in 2006, in which two groups were asked to interview a specific person. To the experimental group, it was suggested before the interview that the interviewee was not speaking the truth (a fact that had not been examined in reality) and the control group was told nothing. At the end of the interview, all the interviewers were asked to rank the degree of eye contact made by the interviewee during the interview (lack of eye contact is considered as a sign of dishonesty). The participants in the experimental group reported less eye contact than the ones in the control group.

In another experiment conducted by the Swedish Karl Ask and published in 2008, the participants were police cadets. They were exposed to information regarding homicide cases, which included clues implicating specific murder suspects. Then, each of the participants was given the file of a suspect. All the files contained evidence (e.g., line-ups, DNA tests, and photograph tests). Part of the evidence pointed to the suspects' culpability, and part of it pointed to their innocence. The cadets were asked to evaluate the credibility of the evidence. They estimated the incriminating evidence as more reliable and used less argumentation for negating it.

From all the existing research, we may point to four main factors, which combined together create the conditions for confirmation bias:

a. Profusion of complex information available to the "judges". The polygraph, for instance, includes at least three physiological measures, and each one of them contains complex information. Moreover, during the examination, at least three series of approximately ten questions are asked. Also, in graphological analysis, as we have seen in Chapter 3, the signs, as well as the interactions between them, are abundant and intricate.
b. Absence of an objective system for quantifying and synthesizing the data. In the absence of such a system, the "judges" rely mainly on their subjective feelings and intuitions.
c. The "judges" have preliminary information regarding the object of their examination. which may be obtained prior to or during the examination. In the case of the polygraph, the examiners have access to the suspects' files and have the information obtained from the initial interview with the suspect. Their impression of the suspect during the initial interview may also influence their a priori hypothesis of whether the suspect is innocent or guilty. In the case of graphology, the examiners have the text content, and in the case of the cold readers, as we have demonstrated, they extract the information prior to as well as during their interaction with their clients.
d. The "judges" begin the examination with a hypothesis inferred from the preliminary information at their disposal. As a result of these four factors, the "judges" tend to interpret the data at their disposal in a way that conforms to their preliminary hypothesis. A single piece of evidence which may be interpreted in several ways will be interpreted according to

the preliminary hypothesis, and when it is necessary to integrate multiple data, greater weight will be assigned to data that support the hypothesis.

The process leading to confirmation bias is an unconscious one; in that, the "judges" who interpret the data according to their preliminary hypothesis do not do it maliciously, for they are unaware of it. We have described thus far one type of confirmation bias – the one relating to the way we interpret data during the process of judgment and decision-making. This is known in the psychological literature as cognitive confirmation bias. But there is another type, even more captivating, relating to the way that the "judges" influence the behavior of the "suspects", and it is particularly relevant to polygraph tests. This type of bias is known as behavioral confirmation bias, or more commonly, "self-fulfilling prophecy". Let us examine a few scientific tests that demonstrate this type of bias.

The American psychologist Saul Kassin and his colleagues conducted an experiment whose findings were published in 2003. In the experiment, which was conducted through the simulation of a police investigation, the "detectives" were divided into two groups. In the experimental group, the detectives were led to believe that the suspect they interviewed was guilty. In the control group, they were led to believe that the suspect was innocent. It was found that in the experimental group, during the interview, the "detectives" selected incriminating questions, used more investigative means, pressured the suspect to admit to his guilt, and decided on a "guilty" verdict more often than the "detectives" in the control group. During the second stage of the experiment, neutral judges (i.e., who were not aware of the detectives' and the suspects' group affiliation) listened to recordings of these investigations (interviews) and were asked to judge the behavior of both detectives and suspects. It was found that in the experimental group the suspects displayed more defensive behavior and tended to behave like guilty persons in comparison to the ones in the control group. The findings show that the initial position of the investigators yields a process of behavioral confirmation bias, whereby their preliminary expectations influence both the investigator's as well as the suspect's behavior. Thus, behavioral confirmation bias may account, among other things, for innocent suspects who will ultimately admit to a crime they have not committed.

The American psychologist Mark Snyder and his colleagues conducted at the end of the 1970s and during the 1980s a series of experiments on behavioral confirmation bias. One experiment included male participants who were divided into two groups. In both groups, the participants conversed with a woman via an intercom. In the first group, the men were told that they were talking to an attractive woman, and in the other group, they were told that they were talking to an unattractive woman. The recorded conversations were analyzed by objective "judges". It was found that the men who had been told they had an attractive interlocutor behaved in a friendly manner and more openly than the men in the other group. Furthermore, it was also found that their interlocutors expressed more self-confidence, more liveliness, more friendliness, and more pleasure during the conversation than in the other group. The self-evident conclusion from this experiment is, again, that the men's expectations influenced the behavior of their interlocutors in a way that matched their early expectations. The American psychologists John Darley and Katherine Oleson also maintain in an essay analyzing the behavioral confirmation bias that the research that has been published in this area demonstrates clearly that our behavior toward others may induce in the other a behavior that matches our early expectations.

In the case of the polygraph (employing the CQT), the examiners' early expectations may influence not only the way in which they interpret the physiological responses but also the choice of questions, their formulation, and the way they are presented to the suspects. Interestingly enough, the potential effect of behavioral confirmation bias on the CQT's outcomes has been acknowledged even by ardent supporters of this technique. For example, in an article published in 1992, the American psychologists Honts and Perry – keen advocates of the CQT – maintain that

> ... an examiner who was motivated to produce a deceptive result might ask over-general or provocative relevant questions, and spend a great deal of time on their review and presentation. Subsequently, this unethical examiner could ask

very narrow, specific, or inappropriate control questions and spend very little time on their review and presentation. An examiner predisposed to produce a truthful result could take the opposite approach, overemphasizing the control questions and minimizing the relevant questions.

Honts and Perry raised this possibility in relation to an unethical and dishonest examiner, but decades of research in social psychology teaches us that honest persons can be unintentionally and unconsciously affected by their prior beliefs. A similar claim is made in an article published by the American polygraphist Stan Abrams in 1999:

> There is a delicate balance that exists between the comparison and relevant questions and many variables can tip this balance in either of those two directions. Too much discussion of one or the other during the pretest, a difference in inflection or loudness when the questions are being asked, any discussion between charts that stresses either the relevant or comparison questions, or any mental activity on one question versus another can weigh the balance in the direction of that particular emphasis.

Thus, even supporters of the CQT acknowledge that it is impossible to determine whether the results of the CQT reflect psychophysiological detection or rather the influence of extraneous information and the examiner's bias.

And yet, of all the practices we have reviewed, the one that best demonstrates behavioral confirmation bias is cold reading, for it is based on a reciprocal dynamic between the readers and their clients. As we have demonstrated, the questions presented by the readers unavoidably influence the behavior of their clients, and their clients' responses, in turn, influence the continuation of the questions' choice as well as the readers' assertions.

It goes almost without saying that confirmation bias presents a threat not only to pseudo-science practices but also to scientific research and experiments in the various social science fields. Researchers have explored this problem following the research of the American psychologist Robert Rosenthal, who showed that the interaction between the experimenter and the participant may impact the findings of the experiment in a direction that matches the early expectations of the experimenter. Rosenthal termed this phenomenon "a self-fulfilling prophecy".

And yet, the difference between the pseudo-science practices and the scientific ones lies precisely in the fact that scientists not only recognize these dangers and admit to them, but they have also developed methods to shield their work from them. Psychological experiments, for example, are conducted in the method termed the "double-blind experiment", whose purpose is to minimize the subjective tendencies of both experimenter and participant. In these experiments, both experimenters as well as participants have no knowledge as to which of the participants belong to the experiment group and which ones belong to the control group. Only upon conclusion of the experiment and analysis of the findings is the group affiliation revealed. Moreover, many of the experiments in psychology are done today with the help of computers (e.g., the display of the stimuli, the analysis of the participants' responses), which is, of course free, of any bias whatsoever.

The self-fulfilling prophecy has ancient roots. It is known in prose, scientific, and philosophical literature as the Pygmalion effect, after the name of the Roman poet Ovid's protagonist Pygmalion. In Ovid's myth, Pygmalion sculpts Galatea, who embodies the perfect woman in his eyes. Pygmalion falls in love with his statue, and so powerful is his love that it animates the statue and turns it into a flesh-and-blood woman. The Irish dramatist George Bernard Shaw adapted a similar theme is his play Pygmalion at the beginning of the twentieth century.

Rosenthal and his colleague Lenore Jacobson conducted a fascinating experiment at the end of the 1960s, which they termed "Pygmalion in the Classroom". The aim of the experiment was to demonstrate how it is possible to change reality as a result of the other's expectations. They showed that when they instilled in teachers of elementary grades an expectation for better results from particular children, the latter really excelled in their achievements. The experimenters hypothesized that if they told the teachers that certain children had a particularly high IQ, the latter would do better than others in their achievements – and this is indeed what happened. Furthermore, these children did better also in objective intelligence tests! It is easy to understand that this phenomenon may also breed detrimental results and not only good ones, for we know only too well what happens to children whose teachers term them problematic, lazy, and so on.

Illusory validity

We wish to remind our readers that the standard definition of tests' validity in the psychological literature, as it has been formulated by the American psychologist Samuel Messick, is the degree of support of the relevant theory and the empirical evidence in interpretations and in the actions derived from the test results.

One of the more important aspects of validity, known in the psychological literature as predictive validity, refers to the relationship between the test results and an external objective criterion, for example, the relationship between the assertion of a polygraph examiner that a suspect speaks the truth and the suspect's being truthful or deceitful in reality. But such a criterion is not accessible to the practitioners whose practices we have reviewed, and so they are unable to assess the accuracy of their tools. Furthermore, the judgment procedures are characterized by an inherent inability to receive feedback from the reality, a necessary requirement in any process of learning.

In contrast, our practitioners know very well what their early expectations were and what their final conclusion was, and as we may deduce from both cognitive and behavioral confirmation biases, there is a high probability that these two will be identical. This congruency creates in the practitioners an illusion that their tools have high validity, for the result is almost always compatible with their early hypothesis. In this context, we remind our readers of the contention of the polygraph examiner that in his 1,500 tests, there was only one misdiagnosis. Because he had no access to the truthful reality (the absence of an objective criterion), this assertion can only reflect the fact that only in one case out of the 1,500 examinations, the result did not match the examiner's early expectations.

Another factor leading to illusory validity, especially in the context of graphology and cold reading (practices characterized by the Barnum effect), is the feedback supplied by the clients. As a result of the Barnum text, that is compatible with almost anyone, the clients react with astonishment at having received an accurate personality assessment and transmit this feeling to the practitioners who, in turn, are strengthened in their belief regarding the validity of their tools. But even when the feedback received from the clients does not support the cold readers' assertions, they tend to explain their mistakes retrospectively, in a way that does not harm their belief. Following is a story sent to us by a friend, which demonstrates this tendency in a rather amusing way:

> During my University days I used to travel in the world every year. During my visit in India I had purchased a beautiful silk painting from an art dealer in Bombay, and when I returned to Israel I hurried to the framing shop in my neighborhood. Behind the counter I was served by a young bearded man who must have been in his twenties. When I told him I'd like to frame a painting I had purchased in India, his eyes lit up. Caressing the silk in the painting, he said to me, "You're a Leo, aren't you"?
>
> "How can you tell"? I asked curiously.
>
> "It's obvious", he asserted, pleased from the interest I displayed in astrology. "The painting, its esthetics, so typical of Leo".
>
> "But I'm not really a Leo", I whispered.
>
> Something cracked in the guy's confidence, but in a matter of seconds he reconsidered, took another brief look at the painting, and said, "Then you must be a Virgo"!
>
> "But", I insisted, "What is it about the painting that makes me a Virgo now"?
>
> "Well", he pronounced, "The composition, the love of blue, this is always a Virgo, no question about it"!
>
> "I am not a Virgo", I responded.
>
> "Don't tell me, don't tell me"! shouted the bearded guy, "If you're not a Virgo, then you must be a Cancer".
>
> "Not a Cancer, I'm something else".
>
> The Cancer was followed by the Pisces and the Pisces by the Scorpio, the Gemini, the Taurus and the Aquarius. Whenever I replied negatively, the amateur astrologer slightly bent his height, until he desperately demanded, "What are you then"?

"I'm a Libra", I admitted, "was born in the middle of October". After a minute or two of silence, the sparkle returned to his eyes. "Of course, of course!! There's no question about it. Look at the size of the painting, at the subject – this wise man, surrounded by the animals, of course you're a Libra"!!

"There are no misses", he explained to me while preparing my invoice. "The stars determine everything, including the kind of painting you buy".

In this chapter, we have reviewed some of the factors influencing the clients' as well as the practitioners' beliefs, beliefs that are responsible for the perpetuation of the practices themselves. And yet, even if our need to believe is unavoidable, and even if our curiosity draws us at times toward the occult, it is possible and highly recommended to keep an open mind without renouncing critical thinking. Let us follow the sound advice that has been attributed to a few scientists, to keep an open mind, but not so open that our brains will fall out!

Notes

1 Dostoyevsky, *The Brothers Karamazov*.
2 In Beyerstein and Beyerstein.
3 Nobel Prize winner in Economics in 2002.
4 We refrain from engaging in an in-depth discussion of these experiments because their relationship to the issues discussed in our book is indirect. Those interested in finding out more about them may find the references in our reference list. Kahnman and his colleagues' book has been quoted over 25,000 times!
5 See the Bibliography.

Bibliography

Abrams, S. (1999). A response to Honts on the issue of the discussion of questions between charts. *Polygraph, 28*, 223–228.

Armstrong, J.S. (1978). *Long Range Forecasting: From Crystal Ball to Computer*. New York: Wiley.

Asch, S.E. (1951). Effects of group pressure upon the modification and distortion of judgments. In: H. Guetzkow (Ed.), *Groups, Leadership and Men*. Pittsburgh, PA: Carnegie Press, 222–236.

Ask, K., Rebelius, A., & Granhag, P.A. (2008). The "elasticity" of criminal evidence: A moderator of investigator bias. *Applied Cognitive Psychology, 22*, 1245–1259.

Ben-Shakhar, G., Bar-Hillel, M., Bilu, Y., & Shefler, G. (1998). Seek and ye shall find: A confirmation bias in clinical judgment. *Journal of Behavioral Decision Making, 11*, 235–249.

Darley, J.M., & Oleson, K.C. (1993). Introduction to research on interpersonal expectations. In: P.D. Blanck (Ed.), *Interpersonal Expectations: Theory, Research and Applications*. London, UK: Cambridge University Press, 45–63.

Dean, G.A., Kelly, I.W., Saklofske, D.H., & Furenham, A. (1992). Graphology and human judgment. In: B.L. Beyerstein & D.F. Beyerstein (Eds.), *The Write Stuff: Evaluation of Graphology—The Study of Handwriting Analysis*. Amherst, NY: Prometheus.

Evans, J.St.B.T. (1989). *Bias in Human Reasoning: Causes and Consequences*. Hillsdale, NJ: Erlbaum.

Forer, B.R. (1949). The fallacy of personal validation: A classroom demonstration of gullibility. *Journal of Abnormal and Social Psychology, 44*, 118–123.

Honts, C.R., & Perry, M.V. (1992). Polygraph admissibility: Changes and challenges. *Law and Human Behavior, 16*, 357–379.

Hyman, R. (1989). *The Elusive Quarry: A Scientific Appraisal of Psychical Research*. Buffalo, NY: Prometheus Books.

Kahnemann, D., Slovic, P., & Tversky, A. (1982). *Judgment Under Uncertainty: Heuristics and Biases*, Cambridge, UK: Cambridge University Press.

Kassin, S.M., Goldstein, C.C., & Savitsky, K. (2003). Behavioral confirmation in the interrogation room: On the dangers of presuming guilt. *Law and Human Behavior, 27*, 187–203.

Lady Globes (October 2012, in Hebrew). No. 169.

Levine, T.R., Asada, K.J.K., & Park, H.S. (2006). The lying chicken and the gaze avoidant egg: Eye contact, deception, and causal order. *Southern Communication Journal, 71*, 401–411.

Lilienfeld, S.O., Lynn, S.J., Ruscio, J., & Beyerstein, B.L. (2010). *50 Great Myths of Popular Psychology: Shattering Widespread Misconceptions about Human Behavior*. Chichester, West Sussex, UK: Wiley-Blackwell.

Messick, S. (1995). Validity of psychological assessment: Validation of inferences from persons' responses and performances as scientific inquiry into score meaning. *American Psychologist, 50*, 741–749.

Risen, J.L., Gilovich, T., & Dunning, D. (2007). One-shot illusory correlations and stereotype formation. *Personality and Social Psychology Bulletin, 11*, 1492–1502.

Rosenthal, R., & Jacobson, L. (1968). *Pygmalion in the Classroom: Teacher Expectations and Pupils' Intellectual Development*. New York: Holt, Rinehart and Winston.

Simon, H.A. (1957). *Models of Man: Social and Rational- Mathematical Essays on Rational Human Behavior in a Social Setting*. New York: John Wiley and Sons.

Snyder, M., & Swan, W.B. Jr. (1974). Behavioral confirmation in social interaction: From social perception to social reality. *Journal of Experimental Social Psychology, 14*, 148–162.

Snyder, M., Tanke, E.D., & Berscheid, E. (1977). Social perception and interpersonal behavior: On the self-fulfilling nature of social stereotypes. *Journal of Personality and Social Psychology, 35*, 656–666.

Stanovich, K.E. (2001). *How to Think Straight About Psychology* (6th ed.). Boston, MA: Allyn and Bacon.

6

A final word

Keith Stanovich emphasizes in his book that in contrast to the common belief that we may consider pseudo-science as a way to amuse ourselves, in which some of us are given hope to their heart's desires while others profit financially, a comprehensive examination of the problem shows that the harm done to our society by pseudo-science is immense and far-reaching. In a complex, highly technological, society, the influence of pseudo-science (as we have seen in the quotes from *Lady Globes*) may expand through decisions that implicate many around the world – we may be influenced by pseudo-scientific beliefs even if we are not, in any way, connected to or aware of them.

We hope wholeheartedly that the explanations we have offered in this book will have the power to reduce the consumption of pseudo-scientific or mystical practices, or at least shed a different light on them. If we have succeeded in making our readers think twice before running to a cold reader in a time of trouble, or refuse to subject their handwriting to a graphological evaluation, or be subjected to a polygraph test, then we have accomplished our goal.

Index

Note: Page number followed by 'n' refers to endnotes.

Abrams, Stan 134
abuse: of need to believe 116–17; physical 84; sexual 92
Allen, Woody 27–8, 32n6
Ames, Aldrich 105
Angel, Shlomo xv
"archetypes" 9
Armstrong, J. S. 119
Asch, Salomon 22, 126–7
Ask, Karl 130
astrological sun sign 43 *see also* zodiac signs
astrology 10; and astronomy 37; and Christian Church 36–7; in Greece 36; overview of 35–7; and science 37–44; Western 37
Astrology: Science or Superstition? (Eysenck and Nias) 42
astronomy: and astrology 37; science of 37

Babylonian astrology 36
Backster, Cleve 81–2, 96, 99
Baldi, Camillo 49–50
Bandwagon Fallacy 116
Baraness, Amos 84–6, 111
Bar-Hillel, Maya xv, 46, 97
Barnum, P. T. 11, 14, 124, 137
"Barnum Effect" 11–14, 42, 124
Bedouin tribes 74
Bearison, David xv
beliefs: popular 117–18; pseudo-scientific 141; spiritual 115
Ben-Shakhar, Gershon ix–xiii, 29–31, 46, 53, 62, 64, 93, 96, 97, 99, 130
Ben-Shakhar, Naama xv
Berossus of Kos 36
Beyerstein, B.L. 49, 54, 138n2
Beyerstein, Dale 49, 54, 67
"Beyond the Rational" 26
bias: confirmation 41, 98, 129, 130–6; in human judgment 118–19; for positive evidence 124

Big Five Personality Inventory (BFI) 109
Bilu, Yoram xiii, xv, 7, 66
"The Black Market" 26–7
"the bogus pipeline" method 107
Bohr, Niels 116
Book of Numbers 74
"brain writing" 50
The Brothers Karamazov (Dostoyevsky) 121
burden of doubt, and incertitude 121–2
burden of proof: regarding validity of theory 128; shifting 128

California Psychological Inventory (CPI) 43
Carlson, Shawn 9, 43
"characterology" 51 *see also* graphology
Christian Church, and astrology 36–7
clients' belief 121–2
clients' confidence 15–16
Cohen, Haim 86
Cohen, Yitzhak 103
cold readers: aim of 7–8; and client observation 6–7; and information gathering 6; and "tellers" of clients 7
cold (psychic) reading 2, 3, 121, 122, 124, 129, 131–7, 134, 136; application situation 14–19; cost of 23–33; described 5–8; and psychological science 10–14; success of 19–23; tarot cards 8–10
Coleridge, Samuel Taylor 28
"collective unconscious" 9
Collodi, Carlo 74
Comparison Question Test (CQT) 78, 79, 94, 122

Concealed Information Test (CIT) 86–90; accuracy of 100–3; CQT *vs.* 90–100, 107–8, 112n6; confirmation bias 41, 96, 98, 100, 129–36
contamination 97
control questions 77
Control Question Test 79, 94, 126
CQT 79–86, 90–103; comparison with the CIT 107; accuracy of 100–3; *vs.* CIT 90–100; contamination 97–100; deduction process 95; lack of standardization 94–5; lack of theoretical basis 90–4; use of countermeasures 96–7; screening 103–8; use of integrity tests as alternative to 109–11
Copernican revolution 37
"correlation coefficient" 63, 69n8
Crepieux-Jamin, J. 50
Crowe, Michael 84
Crumbaugh, James 54–6

Darley, John 133
Davar Aher 45
Dean, Geoffrey 66–7, 118
de Baer, Shiloh xv
decision rule 79
Demjanjuk, John 89
Directed Lie Test (DLT) 86
"Doctor" 20–1
Dostoyevsky, Fyodor 121
"double-blind experiment" 135
"the effect size" 65–6

Elaad, Eitan 73–4
Elber, Lotem xv
"empirical" approach, of graphology 56–8

empirical evidence 47–8
Employee Polygraph Protection Act (EPPA) 105
Ery, Fred 71
Evans, Jonathan 130
Eysenck, Hans 41–2

false memory 84
Fay, Floyd 71–2
Fichter, Catherine 41, 42
Fienberg, Stephen E. 106
flattery 17
Forer, Bertram 11
"Forer Effect" 11, 124
Franklin, Rosalind 117
Frost, David 15
Frost, Ram xv
Furedy, John J. 84, 92

Garfinkel, Harold 21
Gauquelin, Francoise 39–40
Gauquelin, Michel 39–41, 42
Gilboa, Gidi 9–10
gimmicks 16
global evaluation method 81, 95
Goldberg, Ezra 85
"graphoanalysis" 54
graphologists' evaluations 61–8
graphology 2, 3, 42, 45, 123–4, 131, 136; and biographical data 61; and "empirical" approach 56–8; history of 49–51; and personality 53–4; and "theoretical" approach 54–6; use of 52–3; validity of 58–68
Greece, and astrology 36
Guilty Knowledge Test (GKT) 87

Ha'aretz 35, 112n3
handwriting: and personality 53–4; samples, contamination with biographical data 61
see also graphology
Heller, Rahel 84–5
HEXACO 109
Hindus 74
A History of Western Astrology (Tester) 36
Holocaust 89
Hont, Charles R. 97, 133–4
The Humanist 37
human judgment: aim of 121; bias in 118–21
Huson, Paul 8–9, 32n1
Hyman, Ray 5–6, 18, 124, 129; on success of cold reading 6; "the rules of the game" 14–17

Iacono, William J. 103, 108
illusory correlation 119, 120
illusory validity 129, 136–8
Inbau, Fred 78
incertitude, and burden of doubt 121–2
integrity tests: personality-based 109; popularity of 109–10; use of, as an alternative to the CQT 109–11
"Introduction to Psychology" course 11
Israel Society of Graphology 59
"Ivan the Terrible" 89

Jacobson, Lenore 135
Jefferson, Thomas 22
Jones, Edward 107
Jung, Carl G. 9

Kahneman, Daniel 119
Karren, Roland 110
Kassin, Saul M. 83–4, 132
Kibbutzim 53

Kishon, Ephraim 64
Klages, Ludwig 51
Kuo Jo Hsu 50
Kurtz, Paul 40

Lady Globes 26, 122–3, 129, 141
Lapidot, Hana xv
Larson, John A. 76, 77
Levine, Timothy 130
Lieblich, Israel xii, 97
lie detector; *see* polygraph
Lie to Me 125
Lilienfeld, Scott 46, 68n2, 116
Lindbergh, Charles 83
Liss, John 84
Lombroso, Cesare 76
Lykken, David T. 71–3, 76, 87, 89, 105–6, 111n1

McCain, John 46
Mars effect 40
Marston, William Moulton 76, 77
Marx, Groucho 120
Massachusetts Institute of Technology (MIT) 20
Mayo, Jeff 42
Medawar, Peter 116
Meiri, Sandra xv
memory distrust syndrome 84
The Mentalist 125
Messick, Samuel 91, 136
Metzer, Jacob xv
Meyer, Georg 51
Michon, Jean-Hyppolite 50
Minnesota Multiphasic Personality Inventory (MMPI) 12
Mischel, Walter 60
Moshavim 53
Münsterberg, Hugo 76
mysticism 37, 115–38

Nature 43
need to believe 115–16; abuse of 116–17
Nias, David 42
Nisbett, Richard 60
No Lie MRI, Inc. 108

Obama, Barack 46
Ohio Supreme Court 72
Oleson, Katherine 133
orienting response xii, 79
Ovid 135

peer reviewing 48
Persian Gulf 35
personality-based integrity tests 110; and handwriting 53–4
personal responsibility, removing 123–4
Personnel Selection Inventory (PSI) 109
Phenomena x, 42, 47
polygraph 2, 3, 4n2, 46, 52, 53, 55, 71–112, 122–3, 126, 128–9, 131–3, 136, 141, brief history of 76–7; Concealed Information Test (CIT) 86–103; Control Question Test (CQT) 78–86, 90–103; Directed Lie Test (DLT) 86; integrity tests 109–11, 112n10; modern 74–5; R/I Test 77–8; use in screening and classification processes 103–8
popular beliefs 8, 117–18, 120
practitioners' belief 128–9, 138
predictive validity 63, 64, 66, 67, 110, 112n12, 136
Preyer, Wilhelm 50
Proskauer, Julien J. 23–6
pseudo-science 134–5, 141; *vs.* science 46–9

pseudo-scientific beliefs 141
psychological science: and cold (psychic) reading 10–14; "stock spiel" 10–11, 13
Ptolemy 36
Pulver, Max 51
Pygmalion effect 135

Reid, John E. 78–9, 81
Relevant/Irrelevant Test (R/I Test) 77–8, 81
relevant questions 77–82, 92, 93, 95, 96, 100, 104, 133, 134
replicability 48
Risen, Jane L. 120
Rogers, Carl 20, 32n3
Rorschach ink blot 55
"The Rorschach Test" 68n6, 130
Rosenfeld, Peter J. 97, 112n8
Rosenthal, Robert 134–5
Ross, Lee 60

Satran, Shai xv
science: and astrology 37–44; *vs.* pseudo-science 46–9
Second World War 89
self-confidence 14–15, 121, 133
Shakespeare, William 118–19
Shaw, George Bernard 135
Sigall, Harold 107
Simon, Herbert 118, 119
60 Minutes 98
The Skeptical Inquirer 39
Snyder, Charles 12
Snyder, Mark 133
social and cultural influences (conformity) 125–8
Society of American Magicians 23, 25
Spanish Inquisition 74
spiritual beliefs 115

Spook Crooks!: Exposing the Secrets of the Prophet-eers Who Conduct Our Wickedest Industry (Proskauer) 23
staging, attractive 15, 133
Stanovich, Keith 68, 116, 117, 118, 141
star-gazing 36, 39
"stock spiel" 10–14, 18, 22, 25, 124
Sundberg, Norman 11–12
Surenton, Betty 41, 42
Symboliker der Handschrift (The Symbolism of Handwriting) (Pulver) 51
systematic observation 47–8, 59

tarot cards 8–10, 16, 125
Tavor, Eli 85
Tester, Jim 36, 37, 39
test predictive validity 110
Tetrabiblos (Ptolemy) 36
"theoretical" approach, of graphology 54–6
Trattato Come Da Una Lettera Missiva Si Conoscano La Natura E Qualità Dello Scrittore (Treaty on How to Tell the Character and the Quality of a Person from His Handwriting) (Baldi) 49
A Tremor in the Blood: Uses and abuses of the Lie Detector (Lykken) 71
Truth and Deception: The Polygraph "Lie Detector" Technique (Reid and Inbau) 78
Tversky, Amos 32, 119

US Department of Energy 106
US National Research Council 106

validity 2, 3, 8, 39, 41, 44, 47, 127–9; CQT 101, 107, 110–11, 112n12; graphology 57–64, 66–8; illusory 136–8
Vanunu, Mordechai 45, 68n1

Weizenbaum, Joseph 20
Western astrology 36, 37

"willing suspension of disbelief" 28
The Write Stuff 49

Yediot *Ahronot* 85
You Will Meet a Tall Dark Stranger 27–8

Zacharias, Larry 110
zodiac signs 40–1
zone of comparison 82, 96, 99